Comrade of the Revolution

Comrade of the Revolution

Selected Speeches of Fidel Castro

Edited by Manolo De Los Santos
and Vijay Prashad

LeftWord

First published in September 2021 by
LeftWord Books, New Delhi, India
in association with
1804 Books at The People's Forum, New York, NY

LeftWord Books and Vaam Prakashan are imprints of
Naya Rasta Publishers Pvt. Ltd.

leftword.com

ISBN: 978-81-953546-9-6

Contents

Foreword

Fernando Gonzalez Llort

READING FIDEL IS a sublime act of learning. With his speeches, you always learn something new, and it seems that he speaks in the present tense because his ideas are more and more current. Fidel was not only the president of Cuba, but he was also a social educator.

His speeches significantly influence the education of those who read them because they convey political, ideological, and social ideas. They are invaluable, ethical and aesthetic messages that contribute to the formation of values. They are also an essential tool for the work of leftist forces, political parties, community organizations, university professors, and study centres.

This volume compiles transcendental speeches on topics, which are as current as they are essential. Fidel tells us about internationalist missions that will remain eternal as a historical record of Cuba's revolutionary spirit and solidarity, the efforts to develop our industry, and the obstacles imposed by the US to sabotage the supply of fuel. It explains the concept of *special period*—a circumstance in which we had to survive and look for ways to develop ourselves. It highlights the attention that should be given to the peasant sector to contribute to the country's economic improvement through a food program. And he reiterates its importance even in the most challenging conditions, the essential importance of saving socialism and the Revolution.

Throughout these speeches, Fidel also recognizes the complex situation Left movements and political organizations are going through in Latin America, a region he describes in detail, emphasizing the social-ills that still afflict our countries. He does an excellent analysis of neoliberalism and its consequences. In the final speech, Fidel recalls his entrance to the University of Havana and his concerns as a young man of those times. He acknowledges that many of his concerns are the same ones he was still fighting for. He focuses on the threats that loom over the Cuban Revolution and the importance of defending it from within because it can be that Cubans themselves will destroy it.

While in prison, I always considered Fidel's speeches an inexhaustible source of knowledge and guidance. His conviction to win undoubtedly strengthened me and made me face that situation with much more courage.

Fidel's discourse constitutes an ethical and political treasure that shows us the way to true social emancipation and justice. By reading them, you will notice how the imperialist schemes of domination towards Latin America and the intentions of the US government to suffocate Cuba are still maintained economically.

With his permanent vigilance for the present and future of our people, Fidel played a notable role as a popular educator in history. His extraordinary vision showed that without political education, there is no possible Revolution.

Fidel Castro: The Conscience of the Third World

Manolo De Los Santos and Vijay Prashad

THE ROOM WENT silent at the UN's 2001 World Conference Against Racism when Fidel Alejandro Castro Ruz (1926-2016) entered. He took the podium and offered his firm denunciation not only of racism but also of the deep scars inflicted by capitalism. 'The inhumane exploitation of the peoples of three continents', he said in reference to Africa, Asia and Latin America, 'marked forever the destiny and lives of over 4.5 billion people living in the Third World today'. It was this history, he said, that left 'the current victims of that atrocity' in poverty, unemployment, illiteracy, and sickness. These 'calamities', Fidel said softly, 'too many in fact to enumerate here, are certainly awesome and harrowing'. Fidel's words mirrored reality. He would not end there. It was hope that captured his personality, not despondency. 'I believe in the mobilization and struggle of the peoples', he said with great passion. 'I believe in the idea of justice! I believe in truth! I believe in humanity!'

It was hard to contain the applause. Fidel, in his customary green fatigues, took in the adulation. There was nothing insincere about it: the leaders in the room admired the guerrilla. He made statements that many of them believed but had come to set aside, ideas from their youth and their anti-colonial traditions. Never would we hear such honesty from these leaders of the Third World. But their applause suggested something important: Fidel spoke for their suppressed values. His words rang true, even as their articulation would be sneered at by the Global North and their puppets in the Global South. The most severe mockery would be reserved for Fidel's hopefulness, his talk of mass mobilization and struggle. For these puppets, words like 'justice' and 'truth' had been emptied of their content.

Fidel, who spoke for a beleaguered revolution in a small island, stood for suppressed historical forces. Against all odds, the guerrillas of the Sierra Maestra defeated the mafia leadership in Havana and defended themselves from the Yankees of Washington, DC. At the inauguration of the Non-Aligned Movement (NAM) in 1961, Cuba's President Osvaldo Dorticós Torrado spoke in a language that irked the less radical leadership of Gamal Abdel Nasser (Egypt), Jawaharlal Nehru (India), and Josip Broz Tito (Yugoslavia). Underdevelopment, Dorticós Torrado said, can be 'overcome only through a struggle against and by total victory against imperialism'.

Determined that imperialism needed to be confronted, Cuba hosted the Tricontinental Conference in 1966. It was here that Fidel said that his government would 'coordinate support for revolutionary wars of liberation throughout the colonized world'. These were not empty words: Che Guevara was already in the Congo working with African revolutionaries, and Cuban material support would soon arrive at Guinea-Bissau, Mozambique, and Angola in the form of military and medical training. It was Cuban assistance to the militants in these struggles that helped defeat Portugal in its colonies and summon the people of Portugal's own Carnation Revolution against the fascist state in 1974. Cuba's internationalist troops in Angola helped defeat the South African military at the 1988 Battle of Cuito Cunavale, which broke the back of the South African apartheid regime and contributed to its demise in 1994. Cuba did its work and then withdrew. It did not seek to occupy—to get business deals or to create military bases. It came to help, and then having helped, it left.

From Birán to Havana

In April 2016, Fidel gave what would be his last speech at the 7th Congress of the Communist Party of Cuba. He spoke to a room full of Cuban communists, but at the same time—in typical Fidel fashion—to the totality of humanity. Though his cadence had slowed, everyone in the room hung on to each word, carefully enunciated by Fidel's deep voice. Fifty-eight years into the Cuban Revolution, Fidel was still capable of captivating the imagination and hopes of revolutionaries and generating scorn in the hearts of his enemies. He was almost ninety, but he was still self-critical about his path and his journey to becoming a socialist and a communist.

In his final speech, El Comandante—a title bestowed to him in the 1953 attack on the Moncada Barracks—took us on a journey to Birán in the province then known as Oriente, where he was born on 13 August 1926. Oriente is also where the final battles took place between the Cuban *mambises*, the intervening force of the US against the Spanish colonisers in 1898, resulting in the neo-colonial occupation of Cuba by US imperialism. Fidel's father, Ángel Castro Argiz, fought in that war as a soldier on the side of the Spanish. Returning to Spain, Ángel Castro found few opportunities in Láncara (Galicia), so he returned to Cuba, worked in the nickel mines, opened a restaurant, got into the timber business with other immigrants, and eventually became a landowner. Fidel's mother, Lina Ruz González, came from a peasant family. Lina Ruz and Ángel Castro had seven children, including Fidel. Fidel studied in a rural public school in Birán and—because of the privileges of being from a landowning family—finished his secondary education in private Catholic schools.

In 1946, Fidel enrolled in law school at the University of Havana, where he was absorbed into the whirlwind of radical politics through the University Student Federation (FEU), which had been formed in December 1922 by Julio Antonio Mella. Three years later, Mella and thirteen others would form the Communist Party of Cuba. Fidel's political energy brought him into the full range of political activity of his time, from the Committee for the Independence of Puerto Rico to the Committee for Democracy in the Dominican Republic. In 1947, Fidel joined the Caribbean Legion, which gathered in Cayo Confites (Cuba) to launch an assault on the dictatorship of Rafael Leónidas Trujillo of the Dominican Republic. The boat carrying Fidel and his comrades was intercepted by the Cuban Navy at the behest of then-President Ramón Grau, acting under pressure from the United States. In the first of many setbacks to come, Fidel narrowly avoided capture by grabbing his gun and jumping into the water.

For his radical politics, Fidel faced the unimaginative repression of the Cuban police, controlled largely by the security apparatus led by Army Chief—and, after 1952, Dictator—Fulgencio Batista. Fidel's circle included communists, some of them members of the People's Socialist Party (PSP), as Cuba's first Communist Party was called at the time. During this period, Fidel also worked with the Party of the Cuban People (Orthodox), a progressive party with an anti-imperialist and anti-corruption platform. Fidel, engaged with Marxism, drew the younger militants in the Orthodox Party towards a more radical stance. In June 1948, Fidel participated in the political campaign of the Party and Eduardo R. Chibás, its main leader. Chibás came third in the presidential election, ahead of the PSP's Juan Marinello, who would later become a close comrade of Fidel's. Earlier that year, in April, Fidel travelled to Venezuela, Panama, and Colombia to help organize the Latin American Student Congress in Bogota. He also participated in the Bogotazo, a popular rebellion sparked by the assassination of Colombian leader Jorge Eliécer Gaitán in April 1948.

Lessons came hard and fast for Fidel. Batista's military coup of 10 March 1952, bathed in the mystifying rhetoric of democracy, did not confuse Fidel. He condemned it immediately as a reactionary and illegitimate action, calling for its overthrow. Meanwhile, he began to organize a contingent of young workers and students, mainly from the ranks of the Orthodox Party. On 26 July 1953, 160 of them, including Raúl Castro, Juan Almeida, Ramiro Valdés, and Haydée Santamaría, attacked the Moncada Barracks in Santiago de Cuba and the Carlos Manuel de Céspedes Barracks in Bayamo. The revolutionaries expected that their attack would spark a general uprising against Batista's regime. However, that uprising did not take place. Instead, Fidel went to prison and many of his comrades were tortured and killed by Batista's regime. Fidel was put on trial, where he gave the stirring speech 'History will absolve me', which offered an outline of the programme of the Cuban Revolution. Fidel was sentenced to fifteen years in the Isle of Pines, though he only served two years. In prison, he deepened his revolutionary plans as well as his theoretical and ideological formation. A public outcry led Batista to allow Fidel and others to go into exile in Mexico, where they began to plot their return to Cuba.

In 1955, these young revolutionaries formed the 26 July Movement and began to organize across the island. They were soon joined by others, including Camilo Cienfuegos and Ernesto 'Che' Guevara. On 25 November 1956, 82 combatants boarded a yacht called the *Granma*, which landed on the southeast coast of Cuba seven days later. As soon as they landed, the group was attacked by Batista's forces. Those who survived rushed into the Sierra Maestra, which became their base for the next few years. Fidel and the small group of revolutionaries rooted themselves in the peasant communities of the Sierra Maestra and reconnected with their comrades across Cuba after a short period without communication.

On 17 January 1957, Fidel led his first successful assault on

Batista's army at the La Plata Barracks. This would set the stage for several subsequent military victories and for the guerrilla force's emergence as an army of the peasantry against Batista's dictatorship. For the next two years, the rebels deepened their war for national liberation and weakened Batista's grip over the country—despite his backing from the United States.

By the last days of 1958, Batista's troops faced overwhelming defeat. The dictator fled on New Year's Eve, his aircraft carrying as much of the country's wealth as possible. On 31 December, Fidel called for a general strike lasting till 4 January, which broke the regime's back. On 1 January 1959, the guerrilla entered Santiago de Cuba. A week later, Fidel and his 1,000 troops drove into Havana and confronted 2,000 men armed with Sherman tanks, whom he enlisted into the rebel army; every one of them joined and rolled into Havana with their new leader. The Cuban Revolution had triumphed.

Building Socialism

In 1965, Fidel Castro reflected on the triumph of the Cuban Revolution. His thoughts about the subjective side of history—referring, in Fidel's words, 'to the degree of consciousness of the people ... and the degree of development of the organizations of the people'—are worth taking into consideration today, particularly at a time when the world seems to drift further and further away from revolutionary possibilities. On the 13th anniversary of the attack on the Moncada Barracks, Castro shared his strong sense of destiny and conviction:

> Revolutionaries of conviction, who feel a cause deeply, who have a theory and are capable of interpreting that theory in accordance with the facts are, unfortunately, very few. But if and when there are men with such convictions, even though

> they be only a handful, then where the objective conditions for revolution exist, there will be revolution. For history makes the objective conditions, but man creates the subjective conditions.

The Revolution was greeted by the flight of wealth. As Batista fled into exile—$424 million of Cuban reserves were shifted to US banks. The fleeing oligarchy and vindictive US corporations conducted a scorched earth campaign, taking whatever they could from a country that colonial forces had long drained of its wealth. Even before the official US blockade began in 1962, US corporations and banks tried to strangle the revolutionary government. Loans were not forthcoming.

The basic policy of the Cuban Revolution was *sobre la marcha*—to learn by doing. This was because many of the highly skilled workers who had no commitment to the young Revolution fled the country into exile, including three thousand of Cuba's six thousand doctors, for instance. Militants from the revolutionary war joined students and workers to fill the gaps in the state offices. They did not bring the skills of management, but they had enthusiasm. The new revolutionary regime had to answer the basic questions of the people: questions of starvation, illiteracy, ill health, and indignity. If these were not taken seriously and answered with food, education, healthcare, and dignity, the Revolution would falter.

On 13 February 1959, the revolutionary government appointed Fidel to be their prime minister, a post at which he remained till 1976, when he was elected president of the Council of State and the Council of Ministers. Fidel understood that, as Cuba's new government tried to provide even the most basic needs to its population, and as it tried to fund these new programmes with its fair share of the social wealth produced by Cubans, the imperialists would strike back. There was simply no room for even a liberal agenda to be enacted since such an agenda would raise the people's living standards and cut into the profits of the US-based corporations. This is what Jacobo Árbenz experienced in Guatemala when his modest agrarian reform was greeted by a CIA-backed coup in 1954.

Fidel's government moved cautiously to build the basis to use Cuba's social wealth for popular causes. US corporations and the US government behaved predictably: first with outrage, then by attempting to overthrow the government, and, finally, by putting into place a medieval siege—the blockade—against the Cuban Revolution, which continues to suffocate the Cuban people to this day. It was the structure of US imperialism that made Fidel's nationalization of US industries on 6 August 1960 inevitable. Then, on 16 April 1961, as the CIA attempted to overthrow the Cuban Revolution with a landing of mercenaries at the Bay of Pigs, the revolutionary government proclaimed its socialist character.

The radicalization of the revolutionary process drew in the July 26 Movement, the Popular Socialist Party, the Student Revolutionary Directorate, the trade unions, and the peasant organizations, each of them deeply marked by the imprint of this early period. In October 1965, a new Communist Party of Cuba formed from the union of these organizations and elected Fidel as its first secretary and as a member of its political bureau.

The revolutionaries had to build socialism in an extremely adverse climate. The United States, only 90 miles away, put its entire machinery into place to overthrow the Revolution. The withdrawal of skilled workers who went into exile after Batista was overthrown hurt the technical capacity of the government as well as the country's industries, and the absence of sufficient capital meant that it was virtually impossible to diversify an old colonial economy that relied upon sugarcane and tourism. Cuba, a poor country, had to marshal whatever resources remained—particularly the enthusiasm of the people—and rely upon external allies such as the USSR, which played a key role from 1960 to 1991.

But beyond this, the country continued to face grave challenges, the vast majority resulting from the hybrid war imposed by the United States against the Cuban Revolution.

The enthusiasm of the people had to be developed through a deep understanding of the programme and vision of the Cuban Revolution. In 1961, the government conducted a massive literacy campaign, sending literacy brigades into every part of the countryside to set up schools to train the peasants to read and write. This Year of Education, as it was called, lifted the literacy rate on the island to 96 per cent by the last days of 1961, one of the highest in the world at that time.

Brigades of volunteers built schools, and the state expanded the universities, but the biggest classroom was the regular speeches that Fidel gave to massive public audiences. Through these speeches, Fidel came before the people to explain the conjuncture and problems the government faced with honesty and by putting them into historical context. Each of his speeches is a tour de force of explication, a history lesson, a sociology lesson, a political lesson, and even a lesson on literature. Fidel reached back to revolutionaries from an earlier time—Máximo Gómez, Jose Martí, Carlos Baliño, and Julio Antonio Mella—and dug into the data produced by the government. The traditions, experiences, and oral histories of national liberation and Marxism–Leninism articulated by Fidel came alive as he spoke to new audiences engaged in building a socialist experiment just miles away from the heart of the empire.

Two broad lessons come from Fidel's speeches. First, revolutions are not events but processes, and that the long journey before the Cuban people will produce triumphs but also grave defeats. Second, that defeats are not a permanent condition. The revolutionary starts from the impossible and the unthinkable—such as the Batista regime—to create a new situation—such as the Cuban Revolution. But this new period will have its own crises and setbacks, which, if understood clearly and met with discipline, will create new possibilities. New generations of Cubans learned their Marxism not only in the classroom but in public squares, where they cheered on their teacher and his lectures on the current political landscape.

In 1969, Fidel said that many challenges stood in the way of industrialising the national economy, a statement that elicited a rush of volunteers to bring their energy into the process. In the 1980s, Fidel began to explain that there were growing pressures against the USSR, and he warned about the crisis that this would produce for Cuba; Cuba had to deepen its socialist process, he argued, not surrender to imperialism. A decade later, after the USSR had been dissolved and the US circled like a vulture around Cuba, Fidel used the people's heroic resistance as a lightning rod from which to launch a new process of transformation across Latin America. By the 2000s, Fidel led the resistance to neoliberalism, to the 'gigantic casino' of financialization and privatization, as he called it. He launched a battle of ideas in defense of socialist thought and the permanent mobilization of the people's consciousness. The speeches collected in this book carry forward the battle of ideas that framed the last decades of Fidel's life until he left us on 26 November 2016 at the age of ninety.

Debt Strike

In 1983, Fidel arrived in New Delhi to hand over the presidency of the Non-Aligned Movement to India. He was received like a folk hero, the triumphant leader of a Third World in great distress. The debt crisis of the 1980s had ended whatever hope had been kindled from the anti-colonial movements. Finance ministers lined up at the International Monetary Fund and at the various commercial lenders to raise funds for depleted treasuries. The will to fight for another world had been squashed. Fidel had other ideas. He was not ready to bend his knee. What about a debt strike, he asked? What if every one of the NAM states refused to service their debts?

What if they demanded that their debts be renegotiated? Fidel received a standing ovation. But none of the NAM member states decided to follow him. There was no debt strike. Instead, country upon country faced a neoliberal policy slate that cannibalized their resources.

Fidel continued to beat the drum to the tune of Revolution, warning against the direction being taken by the planet's imperial forces. He spoke about the failure of the world's leaders to craft a global response to the perils that face us all: a financial system that had become a casino, a social project that created perilous levels of inequality, a consumption pattern that would devour the Earth's resources, wars that are the child of greed and hunger. Solutions to such grotesque inequalities were needed. They could not be found in apps and microcredit. Much grander thoughts were required. Fidel persisted with that ambition. It was his boldness that allowed so many people to breathe.

'The market has become an object of idolatry today, a sacred word pronounced at all hours', Fidel told the crowd at the Central University of Venezuela in 1999. These words ring true today: in 2016, the richest 10 per cent of the world's population controlled 89 per cent of the world's wealth. This kind of thinking, Fidel said, has 'impaired the human mind'.

* * *

Nothing held Fidel back. When the journalist Ignacio Ramonet accused him of being a dreamer, Fidel responded, 'There's no such thing as dreamers, and you can take that from a dreamer who's had the privilege of seeing realities that he was never even capable of dreaming'.

In 1953, a lieutenant and his squad captured Fidel and some of his comrades. Fidel hid his identity for fear of execution on the spot. The soldiers wanted to kill the guerrillas. Pedro Sarria, an Afro-Cuban lieutenant, walked about calming them down. 'You cannot kill ideas', he repeated, 'you cannot kill ideas'. Later Fidel wondered what made the lieutenant save his life and repeat that statement. The lieutenant was right, Fidel mused: 'Our ideas did not die. No one could kill them'.

Without the long period of struggle and experimentation, Fidel said, 'without the years we had to educate, sow ideas, build awareness, instil feelings of solidarity and a generous internationalist spirit, our people would not have had the strength to resist'. You cannot kill ideas. Fidel, for the Third World, was not merely another leader. He was the mirror of its aspirations. That mirror will never be shattered.

* * *

We are grateful to the following for their solidarity and work that went into the production of this book: Sandra Ramirez of the Cuban Institute of Friendship with the People; Rosa Miriam Elizalde of the Union of Cuban Journalists; Aldo Cruces for the cover design; Sudhanva Desphande, Winnie Chauhan, and the staff of LeftWord Books; Manu Karuka and Layan Fuleihan of 1804 Books; the Secretariat and Coordination of the International People's Assembly; the staff of The People's Forum; the team at the Tricontinental Institute for Social Research (especially Celina Della Croce); and Deby Veneziale.

Can Ideas Be Killed?

Speech at the solemn ceremony in memory of Comandante Ernesto 'Che' Guevara in Revolution Square, on 18 October 1967, during the Year of Heroic Vietnam.

REVOLUTIONARY COMRADES:

It was a day in the month of July or August of 1955 when we met Che. And in one night, as he tells in his accounts, he became a future expeditionary of the *Granma*. But at that time, that expedition had no ship, no weapons, no troops. And it was like this, along with Raúl, that Che joined the group of the first two on the *Granma*'s list.

Since then, twelve years have passed. They have been twelve years full of struggle and history. Throughout those years, death cut short many valuable and irreplaceable lives; but, at the same time, throughout those years, extraordinary people emerged from our Revolution who were forged among the men of the Revolution, and between men and the people, bonds of affection and bonds of friendship were built which go beyond all possible expression.

And tonight, we gather, you and us, to try to express somehow those feelings in relation to he who was one of the closest to us, one of the most admired, one of the most loved and, without a doubt, the most extraordinary of our revolutionary comrades; to express those feelings to him and to the heroes who have fought alongside him and to the heroes who have fallen with him, his internationalist army, which has been writing a glorious and indelible page in history.

Che was one of those people to whom everyone immediately

took affection for his simplicity, his character, his sincerity, his comradeship, his personality, and his originality, even though we still did not know the other unique virtues which characterized him.

During those first moments, he was our troop's doctor. And so the bonds were forged, and feelings of comradeship arose.

He was imbued with a deep spirit of hatred and contempt for imperialism, not only because his political background had already acquired a considerable degree of development, but because he had just recently had the opportunity to witness the criminal imperialist intervention in Guatemala at the hands of the mercenary soldiers who ruined the revolution in that country.

For a man like him, it was not necessary to make many arguments. It was enough for him to know that Cuba lived in a similar situation. It was enough for him to know that there were men determined to fight with weapons to change that situation; it was enough for him to know that those men were inspired by genuinely revolutionary and patriotic feelings. And that was more than enough.

One day, at the end of November 1956, he started the march towards Cuba with us. I remember that that journey was very hard for him since—given the circumstances in which the departure had to be organized—he could not even provide himself with the medicines he needed, and he spent the whole voyage suffering a serious asthma attack without a single chance of relief, but also without a single complaint.

We arrived, we started the first hikes into the mountains, we suffered the first setback, and, after a few weeks, a group of those who remained from the *Granma* expedition—as you know — came back together. Che continued to be a doctor of our troop.

When the first victorious combat took place, Che was already a soldier of our troop, and at the same time, he was still the doctor. When the second victorious battle took place, Che was not only a soldier but the most distinguished of the soldiers in that action, performing for the first time one of those unique feats that characterized him in all actions. Our strength continued to grow, and a battle of extraordinary importance was fought at that time.

The situation was difficult. The information was wrong in many ways. At dawn, as daylight approached, we were going to attack a strongly defended position from the seashore, well-armed and with enemy troops to our rear, not far away. In the middle of that confusion, it was necessary to ask the men for an even greater effort when comrade Juan Almeida took on one of the most difficult missions, and one of the flanks was completely lacking forces. So, one of the flanks was left without an attacking force, which could endanger the whole operation. And in that moment, Che, who was still a doctor, asked three or four men to follow him, one of whom had a machine-gun rifle, and in a matter of seconds, he quickly set out to take on the attack mission from that direction.

On that occasion, he was not only a distinguished combatant, but he was also a distinguished doctor, assisting wounded comrades and wounded enemy soldiers. And when it was necessary to leave that position—once all the weapons were seized and a long march began, harassed by different enemy forces—it was necessary to leave someone to stay with the wounded, and Che remained with the wounded. Assisted by a small group of our soldiers, he took care of them and saved their lives, and later those men joined the guerrilla column.

From that moment, he stood out as a capable and brave leader, the kind of man who, when faced with carrying out a difficult mission, does not wait to be asked to carry out the mission.

He did this during the battle of El Uvero but had also done so on an occasion we hadn't mentioned. It was during the early days when, because of a betrayal, our small troop was attacked by surprise by several planes. When we retreated from the bombing and had already walked a fair distance, we remembered some rifles that some peasant soldiers who had been with us in the first combat actions had left when they asked permission to visit their relatives at a time when there was still not much discipline in our incipient army. And at that moment, the possibility was considered that those rifles were lost.

We remember how, after we had just raised the issue, and during the bombing, Che volunteered and quickly left to recover those rifles.

One of his essential characteristics was the immediate, instantaneous willingness to offer himself to carry out the most dangerous mission. And that, of course, aroused admiration, the double admiration towards that comrade who fought alongside us, who was not born on this land, who was a man of profound ideas, who was a man whose mind was full of dreams of struggle in other parts of the continent and yet, that altruism, that selflessness, that willingness to always do the most difficult, to risk your life constantly.

This is how he earned the rank of commander and chief of the second guerrilla column that was organized in the Sierra Maestra. This is how his prestige began to grow, as he began to acquire his reputation as a magnificent combatant, which he took to the highest levels during the war.

Che was an unsurpassable soldier; Che was an insuperable boss; Che was, from the military point of view, an extraordinarily capable man, extraordinarily courageous, extraordinarily aggressive. If, as a guerrilla, he had an Achilles heel, that Achilles heel was his excessive aggressiveness; it was his absolute contempt for danger.

The enemies try to draw conclusions from his death. Che was a master of war; Che was an artist of the guerrilla struggle! And he showed this countless times, but he especially showed it in two extraordinary feats. One of them was the invasion leading a column, a column that was being pursued by thousands of soldiers through flat and unknown territory, carrying out—together with Camilo—a formidable military feat. But, in addition, he demonstrated it in his fulminating campaign in Las Villas, and he proved it, above all, in his audacious attack on the city of Santa Clara, which he entered with a column of barely 300 men in a city defended by tanks, artillery, and several thousand infantrymen.

These two exploits consecrate him as an extraordinarily capable leader, a teacher, and an artist of the revolutionary war.

However, after his heroic and glorious death, others try to deny the truth and value of his conception and ideas of guerrilla warfare.

The artist may die, especially when he is an artist of such a dangerous art as the revolutionary struggle, but what will not die in any way is the art to which he dedicated his life and to which he devoted his intelligence.

What is strange about that artist dying in a fight? Still more extraordinary is the fact that he did not die in combat on the countless occasions when he risked his life during our revolutionary struggle. And there were many times when it was necessary to act to prevent the loss of his life in actions of minor transcendence.

And so, in a fight, in one of the many battles he fought, he lost his life. We do not possess sufficient elements of judgment to be able to make any assumptions about all the circumstances that preceded that combat, about the degree to which he might have acted in an excessively aggressive manner, but we repeat: if as a guerrilla he had an Achilles heel, that heel was his excessive aggressiveness, his absolute contempt for danger.

It was difficult to agree with him on this, since we understand that his life, his experience, his ability as a seasoned leader, his prestige, and all that he meant in life, was much more, incomparably more, than the evaluation that he may have had of himself.

The idea that men have a relative value in history, the idea that causes are not defeated when men fall, and that the unstoppable march of history can't be detained may have profoundly influenced his behaviour.

And that's true; that cannot be doubted. That shows his faith in men, his faith in ideas, his faith in example. However, as I said a few days ago, we wished with all our heart that we could have seen him as the forger of victories, forging our comrades and the people under his leadership, forging victories under his direction, since the men of his experience, his calibre, his singular capacity, they are rare men.

We can appreciate the full value of his example, and we have the absolute conviction that this example will serve as encouragement and will allow for men similar to him to rise from the bosom of the people.

It is not easy to combine all the virtues in a person that were brought together in him. It is not easy for a person to spontaneously be able to develop a personality like his. I would say that he is the kind of man who is difficult to match and practically impossible to outclass. But we will also say that men like him are capable, with his example, of helping men like him to emerge.

We do not only admire the warrior in Che or that he was a man capable of great feats. What he did and what he was doing, that fact of facing with only a handful of men an entire oligarchic army instructed by Yankee advisers, supplied by Yankee imperialism, and supported by the oligarchies of all neighbouring countries, that fact in itself constitutes an extraordinary feat.

And if you looked in the pages of history, you could not possibly find any case in which someone has undertaken a task of greater importance with such a small number of men, in which someone has undertaken the fight against such considerable forces with such a small number of men. This proof of self-confidence, of confidence in the people and faith in the ability of men to fight, can be sought in the pages of history, and yet nothing similar can be found.

And he fell.

The enemies believe that they have defeated his ideas, defeated his ideas on guerrilla warfare, defeated his views on the armed revolutionary struggle. And what they achieved was, with a stroke of luck, to eliminate his physical life; what they did was to achieve the accidental advantages that an enemy can achieve in war. We do not know to what extent that stroke of luck, that stroke of fortune, was helped by that characteristic that we referred to before of excessive aggressiveness, of absolute contempt for danger, shown in combat like so many combats.

It also happened in our War of Independence. In a fight in Dos Ríos, they killed the apostle of our independence. In a fight in Punta Brava, they killed Antonio Maceo, a veteran of hundreds of combats. In similar combats, countless leaders died, countless patriots of our independence war. And yet, that was not the defeat of the Cuban cause.

The death of Che—as we said a few days ago—is a hard blow; it is a tremendous blow for the revolutionary movement since it deprives it—without any doubt of any kind—of its most experienced and capable leader.

But those who sing victory are wrong. Those who believe that his death is the defeat of his ideas, the defeat of his tactics, the defeat of his ideas on guerrilla warfare, and the defeat of his thesis are mistaken. Because that man who fell as a mortal man, as a man who was exposed many times to bullets, as a soldier, as a leader, is a thousand times more capable than those who killed him with a stroke of luck.

But how should revolutionaries face this harsh blow? How should we face this loss? What would be Che's opinion if he had to make a judgment on this matter? He already gave that opinion and expressed it clearly when he wrote in his message to the solidarity conference of the peoples of Asia, Africa, and Latin America that if he were to be surprised by death anywhere, it would always be welcome that his shout of war reach a receptive ear, and another hand be extended to take up arms.

And that his war cry will not reach just one receptive ear, but millions of receptive ears! And not one hand, but millions of hands, inspired by his example, will be extended to take up arms!

New leaders will emerge. And the men, the receptive ears and the extending hands, will need leaders who will emerge from the ranks of the people, as leaders have emerged in all revolutions.

These hands will no longer count on a leader of the extraordinary experience, the enormous capacity of Che. These leaders will be formed and trained in the process of the struggle. These leaders will emerge from the bosom of the millions of receptive ears, from the millions of hands that, sooner or later, will reach out to take up arms.

It is not that we consider that his death will have an immediate impact on the revolutionary struggle in practical terms, that his death will have an immediate impact on the development of the struggle in practical terms. But it is that Che when he took up arms again, was not thinking of an immediate victory; he was not thinking of a quick victory against the forces of the oligarchies and imperialism. His experienced combatant mind was prepared for a long fight of five, ten, fifteen, twenty years if necessary. He was willing to fight five, ten, fifteen, twenty years, all his life if necessary!

And it is with that perspective that, in time, his death, his example—which is what we should say—will have tremendous repercussions; it will have an invincible force.

Those who cling to a stroke of luck try in vain to deny his capacity as a leader as well as his experience. Che was an extraordinarily capable military leader. But when we remember Che, when we think of Che, we are not thinking mainly about his military virtues. No! War is a means and not an end; war is an instrument of revolutionaries. The important thing is the Revolution; what matters is the revolutionary cause, revolutionary ideas, revolutionary objectives, revolutionary feelings, and revolutionary virtues that matter!

And it is in this field, in the field of ideas, in the field of feelings, in the field of revolutionary virtues, in the field of intelligence, apart from his military virtues, where we feel the tremendous loss that his death has meant for the revolutionary movement.

Because Che possessed, in his extraordinary personality, virtues that rarely appear together. He excelled as a man of insurmountable action, but Che was not only a man of insurmountable action: Che was a man of profound thinking and visionary intelligence, a man of great culture. That is to say. He had in himself a man of ideas and a man of action.

But it is not just that he had these two features of being a man of ideas—a man of profound ideas—and also a man of action. Che embodied the virtues that can be defined as the most complete expression of the virtues of a revolutionary: an upright, righteous man to the fullest, a man of supreme honesty, of absolute sincerity, a man of Stoic and Spartan life, a man in whom it is almost impossible to find a single stain in his conduct. He is, because of his virtues, what can be called a true revolutionary model.

Ordinarily, at the time of the death of men, speeches are made, virtues are highlighted, but rarely—as it is the case today—can it be fairly said, seldom can it be spoken with more accuracy, that a man was a man of virtue when we say of Che that he was a true example of revolutionary virtues!

But we should also add to this another quality, which is not a quality of the intellect, which is not a quality of the will, a quality derived from experience, from struggle, but a quality of the heart, because he was an extraordinarily human man, an extraordinarily sensitive human being!

That is why we say, when we think about his life, when we think about his conduct, that he was a unique case of a very rare man, as he was able to combine not only the characteristics of a man of action but also those of a man of thought in his personality, of a man of immaculate revolutionary virtues and of extraordinary human sensibility, together with a character forged of iron, a will of steel, and indomitable tenacity.

And that is why he has bequeathed to future generations not only his experience, his knowledge as an outstanding soldier, but also the works of his intelligence. He wrote with the virtuosity of a classic. His narrations of the war are insurmountable. The depth of his thought is impressive. He never wrote about anything if he didn't do it with absolute and extraordinary seriousness, with extraordinary depth, and we do not doubt that posterity will remember some of his writings as classic documents of revolutionary thinking.

And so, because of that vigorous and profound intelligence, he left us with countless memories, countless stories that, without his work, without his effort, could have been forgotten forever.

A tireless worker, he did not know a single day of rest during the years he was at the service of our country. He was assigned many responsibilities as president of the National Bank, director of the Planning Board, minister of Industries, commander of military regions, head of political, economic, and fraternal delegations.

His multifaceted intelligence allowed him to undertake any task with confidence and certainty, no matter how difficult. And so, he brilliantly represented our country in numerous international conferences, just as he brilliantly led the soldiers in combat, just as he was a model worker at the head of any of the institutions that he was assigned to run. For him, there were no days of rest; for him, there were no hours of rest! And if we looked to the windows of his offices, we could see that the lights remained on until late at night while he was studying, or rather, working and studying. Because he was a scholar of all problems, he was a tireless reader. His thirst to embrace human knowledge was practically insatiable, and the hours he snatched from sleep were devoted to study; the days that were supposed to be days of rest were dedicated to volunteer work.

He was the inspirer and the greatest promoter of volunteer work, which today is the activity of hundreds of thousands of people throughout the country. He was the driver of this activity, which becomes stronger and stronger every day among the masses, among our people. And as a revolutionary, as a communist revolutionary, as a true communist, he had infinite faith in moral values; he had infinite faith in the conscience of men. And we must say that, from his point of view, he saw with absolute clarity that in building communism in a human society, moral incentives would be the main driver.

He thought, developed, and wrote many things. And there is something that must be said on a day like today, and that is that the writings of Che, the political and revolutionary thinking of Che, will have a permanent value in the Cuban revolutionary process and in the revolutionary process in Latin America. And we do not doubt that the value of his ideas as a man of action, as a man of thinking, of moral virtues, of unsurpassed human sensibility, and of irreproachable conduct, have and will have a universal value.

The imperialists chant hymns of triumph in the face of the fact that the guerrilla was killed in combat; the imperialists sing triumph in the face of the stroke of luck that led them to eliminate such a formidable man of action. But the imperialists may ignore or pretend to ignore that the character of a man of action was one of many facets of that combatant's personality. And if it is about pain, it hurts us not only that a man of action has been lost, but it also hurts that a virtuous man has been lost. What hurts us is that a man of exquisite human sensibility and intelligence has been lost. It hurts us to think that he was only thirty-nine years old at the time of his death. It hurts us to think of how many fruits of that intelligence and growing experience we have missed the opportunity to witness in its full potential.

We have an idea of the magnitude of the loss for the revolutionary movement. Nevertheless, that is where the weak side of the imperialist enemy is: to believe that with the physical man they have killed, they have liquidated his thinking, they have liquidated his ideas, they have killed his virtues, they have killed his example. And they believe this in such an impudent manner that they do not hesitate to advertize, as if it were the most natural thing in the world, the almost universally accepted circumstances in which they killed him after he was seriously wounded in combat. They have not even spared the disgust of the procedure; they have not even spared the impudence of recognising it. They have advertized the right to shoot against a revolutionary combatant who is seriously wounded as if it were a right of the henchmen, oligarchs, and mercenaries.

And the worst is that they also explain why they did it, alleging that the trial in which they would have had to judge Che would have been tremendous, arguing that it would have been impossible to seat such a revolutionary on the bench.

And not only that: they have also not hesitated to make his remains disappear. And be it truth or lie, when they claim to have incinerated his body, they begin to show their fear, to show that they are not so convinced that they eliminated the fighter's ideas and example when they eliminated his physical life.

Che did not fall defending any other interest, defending any other cause but the cause of the exploited and the oppressed of this continent. Che did not fall defending any other cause but the cause of the poor and the humble of this Earth. And the exemplary and selfless way in which he defended that cause is something that not even his most bitter enemies dare to dispute.

And in the face of history, men who act like him, men who do everything and give everything for the sake of the humble, become bigger and bigger every day and get deeper and deeper into the hearts of the people.

The imperialist enemies are already beginning to notice, and it will not be long before they prove that his death will eventually be like a seed from which many men determined to emulate his deeds, many men determined to follow his example, will emerge.

And we are absolutely convinced that the revolutionary cause on this continent will recover from this blow, that the revolutionary cause on this continent will not be defeated by this blow.

From the revolutionary point of view, from the point of view of our people, how should we look at the example of Che? Do we think that we have lost him? It is true that we will not see new writings again. It is certain that we will not hear his voice again. But Che has left the world with a heritage, a great patrimony, and we, who knew him so closely, can be heirs of his heritage.

He left us his revolutionary thinking. He left us his revolutionary virtues. He left us his character, his will, his tenacity, his spirit of work. In a word, he left us his example! And the example of Che should be a model for our people. The example of Che should be the ideal model for our people!

If we want to express how we strive for our revolutionary combatants, our militants, our men to be, we must say without hesitation of any kind: let them be like Che! If we want to express how we want the men of future generations to be, we must say: let them be like Che! If we want to say how we want our children to be educated, we must say without hesitation: we want them to be educated in the spirit of Che! If we want a model of man, a model of man that does not belong to this time, a model of man that belongs to the future, I say from my heart that this model—without a single stain on their conduct, without a single stain on their attitude, without a single blot on their performance—that model is Che! If we want to express how we want our children to be, we must say with the whole heart of vehement revolutionaries: we want them to be like Che!

Che has become a model of a man not only for our people but for any people in Latin America. Che brought to their highest expression revolutionary stoicism, the spirit of revolutionary sacrifice, the combativeness of the revolutionary, the working spirit of the revolutionary, and Che took the ideas of Marxism–Leninism to their freshest, purest, most revolutionary expression.

No man like him in these times has taken the proletarian internationalist spirit to its highest level!

And when one speaks of the proletarian internationalist, and when one looks for an example of the proletarian internationalist, that example, above any other example, is the example of Che! In his mind and his heart, the flags, the prejudices, the chauvinisms, the selfishness had disappeared, and he was willing to generously shed his blood for the fate of any people, for the cause of any people, willing to shed it spontaneously, and ready to pour it instantly!

And so, his blood was shed on this earth when he was wounded in various battles; his blood was shed in Bolivia for the redemption of the exploited and the oppressed, of the humble and the poor. That blood was shed for all the exploited, for all the oppressed; that blood was shed for all the peoples of America and spilt over Vietnam, because there, fighting against the oligarchies, fighting against imperialism, he knew that he was offering Vietnam the highest expression of its solidarity!

That is why, comrades of the Revolution, we must firmly look towards the future with determination. That is why we must look towards the future with optimism. And we will always look to Che's example for inspiration, inspiration in struggle, inspiration in tenacity, inspiration in intransigence against the enemy, and inspiration in internationalist sentiment!

That's why, tonight, this impressive demonstration, this massive demonstration of acknowledgement—incredible for its magnitude, for its discipline, and for its devotion—shows how this is a sensitive people, a grateful people. It shows how this people knows how to honour the memory of the brave men who fall in combat and how to recognize those who serve them. It demonstrates how this people stand in solidarity with the revolutionary struggle, how this people will always raise and maintain the revolutionary flags and the revolutionary principles aloft. Today, in these moments of remembrance, we raise our thoughts, and, with optimism towards the future, with absolute optimism in the definitive victory of the peoples, let us say to Che and with him the heroes who fought and fell with him: ever onward to victory!

Turning Setbacks into Victories

Speech transmitted live through national radio and television on 20 May 1970, about the 1970 sugar harvest during the Year of the Ten Million.

I WANT TO begin by reminding you of the origin of the plan to produce 10 million tonnes of sugar. Since trade relations started with the Soviet Union in the wake of the aggression by the United States, which deprived us of our sugar quota, the Soviet Union began to buy the surplus sugar that the American market had lost. They purchased the first orders of sugar at more or less world market prices. As you know, part of the sugar is sold on what they call the free world market, and another part is sold through agreements between various nations. Sugar prices vary, although agreement prices are generally higher than free-market prices. A large amount of sugar is marketed through agreements.

Of course, given our country's situation at the time, which required bringing all the petroleum and a variety of raw materials and equipment from the Soviet Union, there was no other way to get it other than from the Soviet Union. As a result, our imports increased notably, yet our ability to pay was limited. The quantity of sugar that we could sell was limited, as were some other goods, which were also sold to the Soviet Union when the U.S. blockade was imposed.

Of the products we exported, sugar was number one, followed by some minerals, a bit of tobacco, etc. In other words, sugar, nickel, a little bit of tobacco and rum were our country's main exports, the principal commodities.

Due to the conditions created by the U.S. blockade, we had difficulties trading with other markets. We had difficulties not just acquiring foreign currency but even trading when we did have it.

Therefore, it was in the socialist countries, especially in the Soviet Union, where we began to acquire a large amount of commodities, products, and merchandise needed for our economy.

As a result of those conditions and the needs of a developing nation, we might even say a disorganized nation, as is any country in the midst of a revolutionary process. The trade imbalance with the Soviet Union grew each year. And, at the same time, as our needs for imports for the nation's development increased and had to increase each year if we wanted both to improve the standard of living—even though it was only a modest percentage each year—and to develop the nation's economy, we could see in the prospective analyses of our economy's development that imports were going to increase notably. In turn, exports could not increase since, aside from sugar, the nickel we exported to the Soviet Union had a limit: the capacity of our mining industry. Nickel plants are extremely expensive and require immense investment over a period of years and the time for research and plans before they can go into production.

The rest of our export commodities were also very limited. We had but one possibility for increasing our exports to the Soviet Union, and because of this, we proposed to the Soviet Union that we establish a long-term sugar export agreement. In this way, we could begin to satisfy the growing needs of our economy and, above all, of our development.

Sugar was practically the only product whose export quantities we could increase so quickly. First of all, because we had some underutilized capacity and, second, because many sugar mills could increase their output with relatively small capital outlays. Some of them had received new instalments for greater capacity but had some bottlenecks that blocked an increase in production. But these could be resolved, and the mill expanded with certain capital outlays. We could also increase the length of the harvest.

At the outset, the Revolution's development plans envisioned the export of 3 million tonnes of sugar to the Soviet Union at 3 cents a pound. This is equivalent to approximately 88 pesos a tonne. This meant that the value of our exports was 264 million pesos. When we analysed the need for imports, the difference became increasingly greater for each year that passed.

If we limited our exports, although an export of 3 million tonnes would be considered a considerable amount, and at a price of cents, which was the approximate market price at the time, it would have been practically impossible to establish a solid base for the increase in imports that the nation needed.

So, we proposed a long-term agreement with the Soviet Union based on our possibilities of increasing sugar production. With the Soviet acceptance of Cuba's proposal, it was agreed to increase our exports until we attained 5 million tonnes of sugar. In addition, the price was not 4 cents, but 6.11 cents.

So, in our perspective plans, the value of our sugar exports would increase from 264 million pesos a year to 672 million pesos.

The 3 million tonnes was a plan envisioning a sugar harvest of 7 or 7.5 million tonnes. The export of 5 million tonnes at 6.11 cents a pound would increase the value by an additional 408 million pesos.

The needs of a developing nation are so great that it is scarcely enough to establish a trade that would allow us to satisfy all our needs even with this massive increase.

We must realize that our country consumes more than 5 million tonnes of petroleum a year: the new thermoelectric powerplants, the industries which we have been acquiring, a whole variety of equipment acquisitions, raw materials, and foodstuffs, because we also import large quantities of food from the Soviet Union, especially cereals, including wheat.

This is the reason for planning for the increase in sugar exports. It was most certainly not a whim, nor the desire to establish challenging goals, nor the glory of attaining 10 million tonnes of sugar, but rather a real need. Besides, it was the only possibility our country had. It was the only area where, by making the best use of the land, increasing production per hectare, taking advantage of all infrastructure, extending the harvest season, and making some investments, we could increase our exports by 400 million pesos. This is the economic base, the reason for the 10 million plan.

When we talked about 3 million, it was based on about 7 to 7.5 million tonnes of sugar production. When we spoke about 5 million, we would have to increase the sugar production to about 10 million tonnes. Besides the Soviet market, there were other markets in the socialist camp. Our sugar exports increased. We had to meet a trade agreement we had signed with the Soviet Union, which was highly satisfactory. Other agreements with socialist nations and exports in convertible foreign exchange and domestic needs practically tripled. This is the reason for the 10 million. Some people doubted whether there would be a market for 10 million.

The problem that our country has faced since the relations were broadened with the socialist camp, despite the blockade, is not a matter of markets but one of production. Our country can find markets for any amount of sugar that it might produce. This is the reason for increasing sugar production to 10 million. This required a mill expansion programme. It must be said that 10 million was the maximum, but before that, we had to produce 9, 8, 7, and 6. In reality, during 1964, 1965, 1966, 1967, and 1968 the increase in sugar production was not achieved for many reasons. The drought was the reason in some instances, and in others, the lack of capacity, and crucially, insufficiently qualified personnel to supervise and organize these activities to achieve these increases.

In 1963, we had the lowest harvest in history—of 3,882,000 tonnes; and in 1964, we had 4,474,000. Later, in 1965, we had the highest of that period—6,156,000. In 1966, we had 4,537,000. They increased and decreased in accordance with the drought periods. In 1967, it was 6,236,000; in 1968, it was 5,164,000; and in 1969, it decreased to 4,459,000.

So, in reality, in 1968, we should have produced 8 million, and in 1969, 9 million; it should have increased by degrees. At the end of 1966, a year of low harvest of 4,537,000, a meeting of all leaders in agriculture, industry, and the government was held to agree on adopting a realistic effort, a maximum effort, in order to increase sugar production in the area of agriculture, wind up the 10 million tonne harvest, and recover in the remaining two years the increase that should have been accomplished in the previous three years.

At the time, our country also had more resources available. At this meeting, which took place on 26 and 27 November 1966, we foresaw that, in 1967, it would not be possible to accomplish great increases because we lacked bulldozers and other things that had been purchased and would arrive in the country in 1967. But in 1968, which was already very close to 1970, we would have the equipment and all the other resources to plant, and even though we had been unable to attain our goals in previous years, we had fallen well behind, we would make a tremendous effort to achieve the goal in 1970. Parallel to this plan, we were developing the programme to invest in the industry. We never thought that industry would limit production, but rather it would be an issue of agriculture. We were not producing more sugar, not because of a lack of capacity in the mills, but because there was always a lack of sugar cane. That is, there was not enough raw material to achieve the harvest. Every year there was underutilized capacity, even though we were carrying out the programme with 1970 in mind, at least ending 1970 with 10 million.

The meeting I mentioned was held in Santa Clara over the course of two days, it was broad in scope. Notes were taken of all those long reports and analyses to determine what areas had to be planted with sugar cane, the yields, and areas by mills because there were mills with excess capacity but no land. Others had too much land and very low industrial capacity. Finally, we had to reconcile the industrial data with the agricultural data in order to have sufficient sugar cane to reach

10 million tonnes in 1970. At that meeting, all of the figures were determined: the fields that had to be planted, the sugar cane needed for the 10 million tonnes to be harvested by the provinces, the yields that had to be attained. The meeting was broad in scope and precise in details. That meeting was the starting point for the whole programme. Exciting things were discussed in those meetings, such as the three-year plan and several reports and discussions about the most interesting sugar cane varieties.

Based on estimates at the time, we could see the possibility of achieving the harvest of 10 million so long as we maintained the yields above all else. Of course, we then adopted the whole plan for moving the sugar cane to avoid grinding sugar cane in July when the yields dropped. The entire programme was based on the historic curve: we shut down some mills that were ahead, and that would be completing their season by mid-April, and we took all the measures that were explained in detail on that occasion.

Later, we took additional measures because the situation was one thing at a given time, and then it became more complicated. So, based on calculations, we decided at the beginning of January and the beginning of February that a sugar mill will increase its capacity in mid-February. Still, it turns out that it is the same in mid-February, and April comes, and it remains the same, and it is the end of April. It is the same; then, every additional setback in production in certain capacities forced us to take new steps, new manoeuvres.

On that occasion, we reported on the state of the harvest. We said that the basic strategy was to maintain the yields. At the time, we said that, first of all, the difficulty in the harvest was centred principally in Oriente, Las Villas, and Camaguey Provinces. We said the harvest was going perfectly in the provinces, Matanzas, Havana, and Pinar del Rio.

In some of the provinces, like Camaguey, the problem is not in daily grinding. Camaguey Province has been achieving a satisfactory grinding. Camaguey's basic problem is centred in some mills, which we have called 'critical' and in comparatively lower yields. I say comparatively because Camaguey's yields are more or less on a par with the province's historical yields. However, compared to the yields in Matanzas, Havana, and Pinar del Rio, it was lower at the time.

In other words, while these provinces were getting yields exceeding the historic yield curve, Camaguey was not behaving in the same way. In Las Villas Province, yields are quite good, but there are persistent grinding problems, and above all, problems with some critical mills. And the significant difficulties are centred in Oriente Province.

In the first place, the difficulties in Oriente Province are related to the volume of grinding and, to a certain extent, too, to the yields. The sugar harvest is an activity that is undertaken in 152 different places in the country, and abstract, overall figures have a relative value. To evaluate an overall figure, it is necessary to have an on-site projection at each one of the points where the harvest is taking place.

What do I mean? I mean that on a given day, the grinding could be somewhat lower, but if on that day the mills with the surplus cane and which have problems grinding to top capacity, even though overall grinding is somewhat lower, it is not a major shortcoming. There may even be a high grinding, and we may find that the so-called critical mills have a relatively low grinding. Then, although the progress of the harvest looks good overall, the shortcomings are greater.

Now, there are mills with cane surpluses, and they also have industrial problems. These are the critical mills because mills operating well can be peaked to maximum output, and we can gain time and resolve the problems. Now then, mills with cane surpluses and industrial problems are indeed somewhat of a greater problem.

At the time, I said something about the progress of the harvest in the provinces in terms of the human aspect—the workers; first, let me be specific about Oriente province's problems because they are the most complex. We could see that Oriente Province was achieving daily grinding figures of 9 million arrobas, occasionally 10 million arrobas. This being the case, it needed to achieve a higher grinding figure if it were to have a satisfactory harvest.

Many persons asked themselves what the problem was—whether it was a problem of the workforce; whether it was a problem of industrial difficulties; whether it was a problem of organization; and whether, if Oriente's yields did not behave according to plans, why was this so; whether there was a good cutting program; whether fresh cane was being cut; whether the harvest was well or poorly organized.

I went to the province and stayed there for about two weeks to give first-hand, on-site information about Oriente's problems. I was there in December, noting the problems, the setbacks in industrial improvements and taking a variety of steps to address the completion of the industrial improvement program.

On this occasion, we were able to specify with full objectivity the basic problem of Oriente Province, which so far is not in the workforce, nor the problem of fresh or stale cane delivered to the mills. In short, the problem has not lain in any of these points. Insofar as the morale of the workers in Oriente province is concerned, it is splendid. This most certainly holds true for the cadres and the leaders of the province. The cane is being ground according to a program, and they are fresh when ground. There is a good harvest organization

The number one problem in Oriente is the problem of industrial improvements, something that can be clearly determined. To understand it, we must say that in Oriente Province, with its thirty-nine mills, large industrial outlays were made in twenty of them. I explained what each of the mills had to grind, what the status of each mill was, and the percentage milled up to that time.

All of what was condensed into one paragraph, which reads as follows: The fundamental problem in Oriente lies in the fact that mills that need 11,675,000 arrobas capacity have a capacity of 9,222,000 at present. Of these twenty mills—the most important sixteen—which should have a capacity of 10,673,000 arrobas, have a capacity of 8,218,000 and have ground at 61.56 per cent of their capacity.

In our opinion, the problem of yields now comes first, we said on 9 February, because if we play down the importance of yields and put forth the effort to grind all that cane, we run the risk of waging a battle that is lost beforehand.

Put it this way: A battle must be waged maintaining all the safeguards from beginning to end, to ensure success, to maintain the principle that the 10 million must be defended to the end.

In fact, we believed that in the end, we could be able to ascertain whether everything depended on the yields, the cane that was left, the late rains, or sustained or reduced yields, in the canes we had to grind in June – these would be the canes we were leaving in the higher places where the historic curve was the best.

In other words, we struggled to grind all the cane of the low places early, which posed problems. This was done in consideration of the historic curve and to maintain the hope for the 10 million until the end.

We were gravely concerned about being able to determine mathematically if the 10 million could not be attained because of this problem of the yields at the midway point of the harvest.

This was because we would still have ahead the rest of the

task—the most difficult part—without the hope of the 10 million. Of course, we considered from the outset, from the first moment, that the day calculations showed that the 10 million would not be achieved, we would tell the people. We would inform the people, for if we failed to do it if we maintained the illusion of the 10 million—so the people would work toward the 10 million—it would not be moral; it would not be honest. It would be at variance with the revolutionary principles that must be preserved and at variance with the method of organization that should be followed with the people.

This is the posture we adopted from the outset, though, of course, we did not believe that the hope for the 10 million would be cast aside very abruptly, long before, and not midway through the harvest.

Moreover, if all the measures adopted in February had not been taken, it would have been in March, that is mid-March, that we would have given up the hope for the 10 million.

Those measures allowed us to preserve the hope until the beginning of May that the 10 million were possible to attain. This was because the calculations made in April, in light of the fact that we were suddenly falling below the estimates, plus the accumulated consequences of the low sugar yields, would have dispelled the hope for the 10 million.

Now, observe that I told you that we were exceeding the capitalists' record by 1 million in February. Let us see what happened in the record harvest made by the capitalists. What grinding capacity did they have? In February, March, and April, it became clear that our grinding capacity in 1970 was less than the capitalists' capacity because of all the reasons we had indicated, which fundamentally derived from the industry.

Thus, we see that in 1952, in March, the capitalists ground 1,259,000,000 arrobas, an average of 40.75, I mean 40.15 million arrobas daily. We were ahead of them by 1.86 million through the extended harvest, and we had ground 1.82, pardon, 1.82 billion arrobas, an average of 34.9 million arrobas daily. This was a difference of 5.75 million arrobas compared to the capitalists' daily grinding capacity in March 1952.

We were waging the battle for the 10 million, with a capacity of 5 million less than the capitalists' capacity in 1952.

That was the actual situation. Thus, in February, March, and April, we were grinding and harvesting with a capacity more than 5 million less than what the capitalists had, for in a province like Oriente, which had between 13 and 14 million, we were grinding from 9 to 10 million.

We are barely reaching 9 million tonnes. Whether or not we reach it will depend on how we work. That is the situation at this moment. We must admit that it will be close if we reach it. We must struggle for it, struggle with all our strength. Considering the cane we still have, we will reach it, theoretically. Let us see if this is possible. The slightest difference in our estimate will affect it. We are going to struggle for it. This is the cane we have, with a little reserve. But we must keep in mind the possibility that the drought may be prolonged, that the yield may drop. Measures are being taken to reach the mark.

So, we have lost the battle of the 10 million to the sugar yield. We must say that if it had been possible to obtain a little more sugar—in Havana Province alone if we had been able to start the harvest a little later, we would have produced 50,000, 60,000, or 100,000 tonnes more. Why? Because our estimate was surpassed here where the harvest began on 28 October. If it had started fifteen or twenty days later, the harvest would have ended at the end of May or early in June; we would have had more cane and a better yield. We began the Havana harvest a little too early.

In this matter of the 10 million tonnes, a basic fact is that the people have not lost the battle. We can say with absolute certainty that the people have won this battle; the people have not lost this battle. It cannot be said that nothing has been gained because the battle of the 10 million tonnes has not been won. The people did not lose this battle. We lost this battle. We, the administrative apparatus of the Revolution, we the leaders of the Revolution, have lost this battle.

The people have responded more than adequately to achieve the 10 million tonnes and more. It is we who did not respond adequately.

I believe that it is only fair to clarify this because it is the plain truth. The battle of the 10 million was not lost over the past two years or this year. We have lost it for the past four years. And we lost it unexpectedly because this had never been the principal problem. Our ignorance regarding industrial problems contributed to our inability to foresee several problems, subjective problems, unqualified personnel, and all those things. Even if we had 8 billion arrobas, we would not have won the battle because of the grinding problem.

I also say that certain factors over which we have no control affected industrial production, no one but ourselves have lost the battle. The people were always willing to do whatever was necessary, with enthusiasm. This is unquestionable. And the people have not lost the battle.

Now, yesterday we analysed the factors of two types. How big is the people's effort? How big is the country's effort? What achievement has been made? To explain this with data—the size of this effort—why we said that it was a record that can hardly be equalled, that we would never be able to equal it. Starting from the fact that we have made a large increase over an average 5 million tonne production, that we are by far the world's largest sugar producer, with sugar mills that are eighteen years old—much older than at the time of the capitalists, with over 5 million tonnes less capacity than then, with full adjustments; all this shows the great effort of the people to achieve this.

How should this harvest continue to be called that of the 9, 8 or 10? We will continue to call it the 10 million harvest. Let the 10 million stand, the date, and the entire program, completely. It is the expression that shows what we have accomplished and what we have not accomplished.

On 7 May, in the last check, it was shown that the possibility of achieving the harvest, reaching the 10 million tonnes, was non-existent due to the drastic reduction in some estimates and the situation was growing. There was no longer any way of reaching that, and not only that, but the difference was not going to be 1 of 2 or 3,000; the difference was closer to a million tonne of sugar. Once this situation was obvious, our intention, as I explained to the comrades on 15 or 16 May, more or less, was to tell the people of the situation between the 15 May and the 20 May, in conformity with a previous decision that once we knew that we could not reach the 10 million tonnes, we had to make it public, divulge it. It was a question of basic respect for feelings, elementary loyalty to an effort, and confidence in the people because this would not demoralize the workers. Because no one thought, I never really thought that the hope would be dashed on such an early date, early May. It is now clear that this would have happened in early April if the measures taken had not been taken. Of course, certain estimates and other things which could not be determined then were necessary.

Yesterday's problem was another type of problem, with other characteristics, but we must say that since 7 May what all the comrades of the province, a group of our comrades knew of this problem since the last meeting. This problem was being fought amidst this situation. All of us had to suffer quite a bit when at a demonstration, as the people call it, we were given the slogans' Cuba, Laos, Vietnam, the 10 million are coming along,' or 'Cuba, Cambodia, Vietnam, the 10 million will win.' And we knew that Cambodia would win, that they will be victorious, and in Vietnam, but that we would not reach the 10 million mark.

I might also say to prepare us to strengthen the Revolution in all areas, to strengthen the party. The mass organizations are very important, because in this extraordinary effort of raising percentages, which I noted today, in eighteen months, was at the price of launching the whole party into the task of planting 40,000 caballeria of cane, which means that we now have some 40,000 more caballerias of cane than we had two years ago and that there are new varieties there, better varieties. Besides this, we had to launch the party into this task, concentrating on this, so the political tasks were neglected to a certain extent. Work with the masses was neglected. A task of this nature introduces elements of administration rather than leadership, and then an emergency situation leads always to the habit of rather doing things administratively because we put the whole party into administrative work, administrative in agriculture, administrative in industry. We wanted to strengthen the administrative machinery in agriculture, and we have some 200 university-level technicians.

They have been working for years—economists, engineers, comrades—to strengthen the national and provincial administrative machinery. The administrative machinery must be strengthened because the party is supported in its leadership function insofar as the administration is concerned.

In these years, in order not to waste a day, in all these months, the ceremonies—the celebration for 26 July, 1 January, all these events—at which the people gather, and express themselves, were suspended for the sake of production, for the sake of the battle for 10 million.

At the same time, the work of the mass organizations was being neglected. We must return to all of those questions raised with the criticism of sectarianism—how the party must work, what the mass organizations are, what importance they have—because the party is not a mass organization. The party is a selection from these. The party is the vanguard, so that if we transform it into the mass, it may one day become in the communist society, party, mass, state, and other things, but in this phase, it is still a selection. It must continue to be supported by the best values of our workers, and the party must serve and develop the mass organizations as it was proposed. It should not be a mass organization. Mass organizations are needed and basic, but when the party is turned into a mass organization, it is harmed, invalidated, liquidated in quality and form. Now the party is the advance guard.

There is also the advanced movement. It is magnificent; it is something new, good, another formidable movement. But basically, there remain those who are not of the party nor the advanced movement. We must work on this. There remain the organizations that must include all the workers. At a certain moment, if a role has been interpreted badly, reminiscent of the past, if errors have been committed, if something has been badly interpreted, all of this means that errors must be corrected. Guidance must be given, definitions must be made, and the role which belongs to the worker's organizations which include all the masses, must be established. This role must be strengthened in the factory, the party, the vanguard, the union. If anyone thinks he does not like the word, we have no reason for changing it. We do not change the word 'army'. We do not change the word 'plane' when it passes from reactionary enemy hands to revolutionary hands. Sometimes it might be good to change the word. We do not change the word 'government'. We do not change this. So, the labour unions must be strengthened.

The mass organizations like the Women's Federation, the Committees for the Defense of the Revolution (CDR), the peasant organizations demonstrated their strength and established, helped, strengthened the spirit of struggle, and directed the people. The strengthening of the mass organizations is one of the political tasks we must fulfil because first of all, in almost 24 months, between 18 of planting and 6 of the sugar harvests, or 8 of the harvest making 26 months in all, political work has been neglected. And this is the only role of the party. The political machinery must be strengthened.

The party does not administer—it guides, it directs, it inspires, it supports, it guarantees—the fulfilment of the plans of the leadership of the Revolution everywhere. To strengthen the administrative machinery, strengthen the mass organizations and above all, to strengthen the party, these are problems that I think it is necessary and proper to point out on this occasion. Often in the task of administration, there have not been enough cadres, and here we have a cadre of the youth, yet we need more cadres. We need mass organizations to be stimulated. They are an instrument of the Revolution, they are the support of the party, the bulwark of the party and the Revolution, and we must develop them down to the children pioneers, who also took part in this battle and impressed everyone with their action.

This same battle waged by the people teaches us the need to pay attention to all those factors. We have seen the degree of closeness everyone has. From the various sectors of scientists, actors, cane cutters, and all the people represented.

From the degree of closeness and conscience that we have seen, the chasm between the Revolution and counter-revolution widens even more. The definitions are increasingly becoming clearer and more precise. And the third slogan is 'turn setbacks into victory!'

That is the energetic, worthy slogan of our people, to genuinely turn setbacks into true victories! To get more of the setback than what victory would have given us in terms of the concern to improve our work, in the sense of responsibility, duty, dedication, and more wholehearted and more absolute commitment to the task of the Revolution.

And to perform and strive for now, over the next few months, the forthcoming year, and henceforth, to draw much more from the setback than what we would have drawn from the victory.

This is what we understand by turning a setback into victory. I am absolutely certain that we will be able to this setback into victory.

When an Energetic and Potent People Cry, Injustice Trembles!

Speech at the memorial service for the victims of the act of terrorism against the Cubana Airline's plane destroyed in flight on 6 October, given in Revolution Square, Havana, 15 October 1976, during the Year of the 20th Anniversary of the Granma.

IN SORROW, MOURNING, indignation, we meet today in this historic square to bid farewell, however symbolically, to the remains of our comrades assassinated in the brutal act of terrorism perpetrated against a civilian plane in flight with seventy-three persons aboard, fifty-seven of them Cubans. Most of the remains lie in the unfathomable ocean depths, without the tragedy having left the relatives even the consolation of their bodies. It has been possible to retrieve the physical remains of only eight Cubans. They thus become the symbol of all those who died, the sole material remains we will bury in our land of those fifty-seven healthy, vigorous, enthusiastic, selfless, young compatriots. Their average age was barely thirty, although their lives had nevertheless already been immensely rich in terms of their contribution to work, studies, sports, to their family and friends, and to the Revolution.

When we read each one's biography, we see that each page is filled with the splendid service to the country their lives represented. The captain of the plane had been elected National Work Hero this very year. Many had earned the 20th Anniversary Medal. Several crew members had provided various internationalist services, and the athletes had just finished writing a brilliant and insuperable page in sports history by winning all the gold medals in the regional fencing competition that had just been held in Caracas. Many were members of the Communist Youth or the Party; all were outstanding in their activities, and each one of them had been a lucid example of how devotion to study, achievement, work, and the fulfilment of duty is the essential characteristic in our citizenry today.

They weren't millionaires on a pleasure trip; they weren't tourists with time and money to visit other countries; they were humble workers, students, and athletes performing the tasks their country had given them, with modesty and devotion.

Among the passengers were eleven Guyanese youth, six of them selected to study medicine in Cuba. Lives lost of men whose destiny was to save lives in their underdeveloped and poor country. Five dedicated citizens of the Democratic People's Republic of Korea also died, representatives of a people who have been victims of United States aggression for so long, who were visiting Latin American countries on a friendship trip.

The plane was destroyed in flight by an explosion a few minutes after it had taken off from the Barbados airport. With indescribable heroism, the brave and expert pilots of the plane made a supreme effort to land, but the burning and almost destroyed craft could only remain aloft a few more minutes. However, they had enough time and fortitude to explain that there had been an explosion aboard, that the plane was on fire, and that they were trying to land. It is unimaginable what an impact the explosion and fire must have had on the passengers and crew enclosed in an airplane at an altitude of approximately six thousand meters.

Some imperialist news agencies immediately mentioned a possible mechanical failure, but everything the pilot transmitted to the Barbados airport was taped. More evidence was immediately added. Two individuals with Venezuelan documents had boarded the plane in Trinidad and left it in Barbados before the accident;

almost immediately after the plane blew up in the air, they boarded a return flight to Trinidad, where they checked into the most luxurious hotel without any luggage at all. At the request of the Barbados authorities, whose suspicions had been aroused, they were arrested.

The investigations begun by the police of both countries immediately produced evidence strongly indicating that they were the physical perpetrators of the sabotage.

Because of the documents they used, the Venezuelan authorities quickly became apprised of the events involved in the investigation. On the following day, 7 October, in a cable of condolence to Cuba, the president of Venezuela, Carlos Andrés Pérez, described the deed as an abominable crime. Later, the prime minister of Barbados used similar terms publicly when he spoke at the United Nations' headquarters. The fact that those governments whose officials had access to the most immediate and important sources of information, the detainees themselves, the circumstances surrounding their behaviour and their documents, labelled the act as one of terrorism, was already very significant in itself.

Although after receiving the initial information, the government of Cuba had no doubt about what caused the tragedy, it refrained from making any statement, instead waiting to carefully analyse the news that it was receiving and the background and reports, some of which was public and others confidential.

At first, the real identity of the detainees was not precisely known. It was said that perhaps the documents were false. The names Freddy Lugo and José Velázquez were released, it was said that the latter also called himself José García, and that he held more than one passport. Later, the press also reported that the Venezuelan consul had talked with the detainees for five hours and that the United States Ambassador in Barbados had hurriedly left for Washington. Nevertheless, news surrounding the detainees and other details and circumstances of interest were tightly guarded.

On 9 October, the government of Venezuela stated that Freddy Lugo was a Venezuelan citizen and that investigations were proceeding to identify José Velázquez or José García.

On 10 October, several absolutely reliable sources in Venezuelan press circles, indignant at the monstrous crime, sent Cuba highly important reports. The reports revealed that a photographer from the newspaper *El Mundo*, Hernan Ricardo, had been seen two weeks earlier with Félix Martínez Suárez, a well-known enemy of the Cuban Revolution, and two other individuals, that Hernan Ricardo was inseparable from Freddy Lugo, and that two days after the explosion of a bomb in the Cubana Airline's office in Panama, Hernan Ricardo had arrived at Maiquetía airport on a flight from that country. The report also had proof that said person held three passports, one of them in the name of José Velázquez and that in the very editorial offices of *El Mundo* newspaper, he had bragged that he knew a Cuban plane would be blown up in Barbados.

But the most essential and important point these well-informed Venezuelan sources communicated to us, was that it was widely known that Hernan Ricardo was a CIA agent, that he often handled reports from the agency, and that, while earning a relatively modest salary of 1,600 bolívares, he had a car that cost 40,000 and an apartment that cost 100,000. Some people had also heard him talking with Freddy Lugo about the explosives courses that they were taking. And because of all this background, they suspected that the other person arrested, who claimed to be José Velázquez, was Hernan Ricardo.

Two days later, on 12 October, the government of Venezuela officially announced that the second detainee, José Velázquez, was really Hernan Ricardo.

This explained everything.

Based on the data that we have accumulated, we must add to the reports from Venezuela: Félix Martínez is a well-known CIA agent.

News reports from Venezuela speak about fabulous amounts of money given to the physical perpetrators of the deed.

Venezuelan territory was unquestionably used to work out the final phase of the sabotage, and citizens of that country were undoubtedly the physical perpetrators of the horrible crime. But this in no way leads us to confuse the issue.

It is true that there is a group of well-known Cuban counter-revolutionaries in Venezuela who have a degree of access to specific political circles, who are implicated in imperialism's terrorist plans against our country, and some of them likely had a hand in the events. But we don't harbour the slightest doubt that the government of Venezuela has absolutely nothing to do with the United States' aggressive plans against Cuba, that its attitude toward our country has been honest, that just as President Carlos Andrés Pérez himself has promised, it will make an exhaustive investigation concerning the involvement of Venezuelan citizens or residents of the country in the repugnant events, and will demand that responsibility for the use of Venezuelan territory as a base for terrorist acts of aggression be placed where it belongs.

The recruitment of citizens and the use of other countries' territories to carry out acts of that nature are methods typical of the CIA.

In the beginning, we had doubts as to whether the CIA had directly organized the sabotage or had carefully executed it through its cover organizations made up of Cuban counter-revolutionaries; we are now decidedly inclined toward the first theory. The CIA participated directly in the destruction of the Cubana Airline's plane in Barbados.

The most repugnant aspect of this case is the use of mercenaries who, for money, are capable of ending in a few seconds the precious lives of seventy-three defenceless persons, people who had been their fellow passengers on the plane only a few minutes earlier.

In recent months, the government of the United States, resentful at Cuba's contribution to the defeat the imperialists and racists suffered in Africa, has unleashed a series of terrorist actions against Cuba, accompanied by brutal threats of aggression. This campaign has been intensified day by day and has been directed chiefly against our diplomatic headquarters and our airlines.

On 9 July of this year, in Kingston, Jamaica, only a few weeks before the plane sabotage in Barbados, a powerful bomb exploded in a cart carrying luggage to the Cubana Airline's flight leaving for Cuba. The bomb did not explode while the plane was in flight because its arrival had been delayed.

On 2 October of this year, four days before the plane sabotage in Barbados, the counter-revolutionary journalist Llano Montes, who has reason to be well informed about those events, wrote in the *Caracas El Mundo* that a plastic dynamite bomb had been fastened under the wing of a Cubana Airline's plane in Barbados and had been loosened by a little stream of gasoline when the plane went down the runway to start its flight. He added that an airport security employee found the plastic dynamite on the ground, deactivated it, and took it to the office, where it disappeared without his superiors being informed of the facts.

Not only have all the Caribbean and Central American states that maintain relations with our country been used in the terrorist acts perpetrated against Cuba—Mexico, Panama, Colombia, Jamaica, Barbados, Trinidad and Tobago, Venezuela—but also other neighbouring states such as the Dominican Republic and Costa Rica, where the terrorists live, move, and organize, as well as in the United States, Puerto Rico, Nicaragua, and Chile where they are based and act openly with official support. In expanding these activities, imperialism has shamelessly violated the sovereignty and the laws of many countries in the region.

The perpetrators of these crimes move everywhere with impunity; they have inexhaustible funds; they carry United States passports as naturalized citizens of that country, or real or false documents from other countries; and they use the most sophisticated methods of terror and crime.

Who, if not the CIA, with the sanctuary of established imperialist domination and impunity in this hemisphere, is capable of such deeds?

An important aspect is the Central Intelligence Agency's close association with the tyrannies of Nicaragua and Chile in order to carry out these plans.

While the territories of Nicaragua and Guatemala have served as a base for armed aggressions against Cuba even during the mercenary attack on the Bay of Pigs, and later pirate attacks launched from bases in Miami, Puerto Rico, the Dominican Republic, and Costa Rica, today the same groups of counter-revolutionary types are being used by Somoza and Pinochet as well, according to the specific purposes of each, not only against Cuba, but also against Panama, Jamaica, Guyana, the Chilean popular movement, and other Latin American progressive movements.

It is a well-known fact that every time the CIA has concocted a plan of action against Cuba, at the time of the Bay of Pigs or later by perpetrating the interminable chain of pirate attacks, and organising and directing subversive actions and arms deliveries, it has always, on every occasion, disguised its activities under the cloak of various Cuban counter-revolutionary organizations. It is impossible to recall the number of names and initials this shady Yankee institution has created.

Last June, a group of terrorist counter-revolutionary organizations, all of them located inside the United States, including the so-called National Liberation Front of Cuba, Cuban Action, Cuban Nationalist Movement, Brigade 2506, and F-14, chiefly composed of individuals who have worked for the CIA for a number of years and have received training from it, met in Costa Rica to create the so-called Command of United Revolutionary Organizations (CORU).

These groups not only act freely and with impunity from United States territory, but through CORU, their principal leaders are closely linked to CIA activities against Cuba.

The actions are not always carried out by members of these cover groups. Many times, the CIA does the dirty work by other means, and the events are then attributed to the organizations that have been created.

In the United States, these groups publicly proclaim their crimes and announce new acts of vandalism.

In August 1976, an alleged war communique was printed in a counter-revolutionary newspaper published in Miami, which, after describing how they blew up an automobile in front of the Cuban Embassy in Colombia and destroyed the Cubana Airline's offices in Panama, stated at the end: 'Very soon we will attack airplanes in flight...' and was signed by the five previously mentioned terrorist organizations located in Miami.

In another Miami newspaper, on 19 September of this year, we read a detailed description by CORU of the attempt to kidnap the Cuban consul in Mérida and the assassination of the fishing technician Artagnán Díaz Díaz together with the plan to dynamite the Cuban Embassy in Mexico. Two of the assassins had flown from Miami to Mexico with United States passports to do the work and were arrested in that country following the crime. A third returned to the United States, escaping Mexican justice.

In another of the malicious articles published in Miami, on 9 September 1976, there is a picture spread of a so-called congress of the terrorist organization Brigade 2506 held in that city. The same publication includes the photo of the tyrant Somoza making the closing speech and, with him, a Yankee congressman, Claude Pepper.

Another publication printed the photo of an assembly of those counter-revolutionary groups presided over, according to the picture caption, by Julio Durán, Chilean Ambassador to the United Nations, the Mayor of Miami, Maurice Ferrer, Chilean Consul General in Miami, Colonel Eduardo Sepúlveda, and US Congressman Tom Gallagher.

What is strange about the fact that now CORU claims

responsibility, through the news agency AP, for the repugnant feat of having dynamited a passenger plane in flight with seventy-three people aboard?

Why should it be strange for these same groups to assassinate former Chilean Minister Orlando Letelier, whose death infuriated Latin American and world opinion?

Reviewing the terrorist acts perpetrated against Cuba since the United States government launched its insolent threats against our country, we have the following:

6 April 1976. Two fishing boats, Ferro 119 and Ferro 123, are attacked by pirate launches coming from Florida, causing the death of the fisherman Bienvenido Mauriz and causing serious damage to the boats.

22 April. A bomb is placed in the Cuban Embassy in Portugal causing, the death of two comrades and seriously wounding several others, and completely destroying the premises.

5 July. The Cuban Mission to the United Nations is the object of an explosives attack, causing important material damage.

9 July. A bomb explodes in the cart carrying luggage to a Cubana Airline's flight in the Jamaican airport moments before boarding time.

10 July. A bomb explodes in the British West Indies Airways office in Barbados, which represents Cubana Airline in that country.

23 July. A technician from the National Fishing Institute, Artagnán Díaz Díaz, is assassinated in an attempt to kidnap the Cuban consul in Mérida.

9 August. Two officials of the Cuban Embassy in Argentina are kidnapped and have disappeared without a trace.

18 August. A bomb explodes in the Cubana Airline's office in Panama, causing considerable damage.

6 October. The Cubana Airline's plane is destroyed in flight with seventy-three persons aboard.

As is evident, in just two months, two extraordinarily serious sabotages were organized against Cuban planes on international flights filled with passengers, one of which was fatal.

Behind these deeds stands the CIA. And almost without exception, on all occasions, the terrorist organizations located inside the United States and acting with impunity in that country's territory, essentially the five that form the so-called CORU, claimed responsibility for them.

I wish to recall that the CIA has instigated criminal methods that have increasingly affected the international community in recent years. The CIA plotted and encouraged skyjacking for use against Cuba during the early years of the Revolution; the CIA plotted pirate attacks from foreign bases in its aggressive policy against Cuba; the CIA plotted the destabilization of foreign governments; the CIA revived for modern times the deplorable policy of plotting and committing assassinations of leaders of other countries; and the CIA has now plotted the ominous scheme to blow up civilian airplanes in flight. The world community must be aware of the gravity of these events.

Even after the United States Senate investigated and publicly acknowledged the countless CIA plots to assassinate leaders of the Cuban Revolution and its dedication to that end for a number of years, the United States government has given the Cuban government no explanation of those events, nor has it in any way apologized.

We suspect that the United States government has not given up such practices. On 9 October, only three days after the criminal sabotage in Barbados, a message sent by the CIA to an agent in Havana was intercepted. That message, transmitted from the CIA's central headquarters in Langley, Virginia, says in part: 'Please inform at the earliest opportunity any data concerning Fidel's attendance at the ceremony for the first anniversary of Angola's independence, 11 November. If he's going, try to get a complete itinerary for Fidel's visit to other countries on the same trip.'

Another order, dated earlier, says: 'What is the official and specific reaction concerning bomb attacks against Cuban offices abroad? What are they going to do to avoid them and prevent them? Who do they suspect is responsible? Will there be reprisals?'.

We hope the United States government does not dare deny the truth of these instructions, from the CIA's main office and many others, sent to the same person in flagrant acts of espionage. We have the code, the ciphers, and absolute proof that these messages are authentic. In this particular case, the presumed agent recruited by the CIA has kept the Cuban government informed, from the very beginning and for ten years, of all details of every contact he had with it, the equipment, and instructions he received. The CIA thought the agent had succeeded in placing a modern electronic micro transmitter given to him for that purpose in no less a place than the office of Comrade Osmany Cienfuegos, Secretary to the Executive Committee of the Council of Ministers. Hence the CIA's certainty in assuming it would receive, in plenty of time, the pertinent information of any trip abroad made by the Cuban prime minister.

Those who believe the CIA has changed one iota, because of the denunciations its hair-raising actions have caused within United States society itself, are deeply mistaken. Its methods will simply become more subtle and more perfidious.

Why did the CIA want to know the exact itinerary of the prime minister's possible trip to Angola and other African countries in honour of 11 November? Why did it want to know what measures would be taken to avoid and prevent terrorist acts?

Considering the importance of this fact and the enlightening value it has in terms of the CIA's conduct and activities, we have considered it appropriate to reveal it publicly, although this implies the sacrifice of a valuable source of information.

Three years ago, the Cuban government signed an agreement with the United States government on air and maritime piracy and other crimes. This was an important contribution on the part of our country to the solution of the serious world problem of skyjacking.

The Cuban government demanded no conditions whatsoever for signing that agreement, not even the end of the criminal economic blockade the United States government has maintained against our country. Moreover, without any legal obligation whatsoever, Cuba returned to a United States enterprise the two million dollars some skyjackers had brought with them, and that was confiscated by our authorities.

On one occasion, Cuban authorities at the Rancho Boyeros airport saved the lives of many United States citizens leaving Florida when the plane had to make an emergency landing after United States police had shot up the tires in a futile attempt keep it on the ground. We would have behaved in precisely the same way under any similar circumstances, strictly for humanitarian reasons.

How different from the brutal conduct of those who armed the assassins and inspired the destruction of our plane in Barbados!

Cuba has never and will never propagandize in favour of skyjackers and is prepared to collaborate realistically with any responsible government in the struggle against air piracy and terrorism.

But the United States government has been incapable of fulfilling the spirit and letter of the agreement signed with Cuba in February 1973.

After the unpunished assassination of a Cuban fisherman and the destruction of two boats by a pirate attack off the Florida coasts, we warned the United States government that if events such as those were repeated and their perpetrators were not properly punished, the agreement would no longer be valid.

There was no reply. The crime was neither investigated nor punished.

The agreement signed between the governments of the United States and Cuba on 15 February 1973 cannot survive this brutal crime.

The Cuban government finds it necessary to cancel it and will, therefore, so inform the United States government this afternoon. According to the textual terms of the agreement, at any time during the period of its validity and by written renunciation made six months beforehand, one of the parties can communicate to the other its decision to end the agreement. Strictly adhering to the agreement and proceeding to notification of its renunciation today, 15 October 1976, said the agreement would have validity only up to 15 April 1977, and we will not again sign any such agreement with the United States until the terrorist campaign unleashed against Cuba is definitively terminated, effective guarantees against these actions are made to our people, and there is an end to United States acts of hostility and aggression against Cuba. There can be no collaboration of any kind between an aggressor and a country under attack.

If after 15 April 1977, when the validity of the agreement ends, should any US commercial plane be detoured to Cuba, the plane, as well as the crew and passengers, will be given every possible means to return immediately to their country.

Cuba will never encourage skyjacking, nor will it be tolerant with its perpetrators; but Cuba cannot maintain virtually unilateral commitments to return or punish such perpetrators with a government that bears the basic responsibility for this infamous terrorist offensive against our country.

The agreements of a similar nature signed with Canada, Mexico, Colombia, and Venezuela, will remain fully valid.

Cuba is also prepared to collaborate with Mexico, Panama, Venezuela, Colombia, Jamaica, Trinidad and Tobago, Guyana, Barbados, and other Caribbean and Central America countries capable of acting in good faith in any joint measures considered appropriate in combating these crimes.

Cuba is even ready to discuss with the United States, whichever government is elected in November, a solution to these problems; but I repeat, only on the basis of the definitive halting of all acts of hostility and aggression against our country.

We might ask ourselves what the purpose of these crimes is? To destroy the Revolution? That is impossible. Faced with the cowardice and monstrosity of such crimes, the people are inflamed, and every man and woman become a fervent and heroic soldier prepared to die.

The Revolution has taught us all the idea of human fraternity and solidarity. It has made us all the most profound brothers among whom the blood of one belongs to all and the blood of all belongs to each of the others. So, the sorrow is everyone's, the mourning is everyone's; but the invincible strength of millions of people is our strength. And our strength is not only the strength of one people, but also the strength of all the peoples who have now freed themselves from slavery and of all those in the world who struggle to eliminate exploitation, injustice, and crime from human society.

In short, our strength is the strength of patriotism and the strength of internationalism. The ideas we fight for are the banner for the world's most honest and worthy men and women and the certain and victorious emblem of the world of tomorrow.

Imperialism, capitalism, fascism, neocolonialism, racism, man's brutal exploitation of man in all its forms and manifestations, are approaching their end in humanity's history, and their maddened lackeys know it; that is why their reactions are ever more desperate, more hysterical, more cynical, more impotent. Only this can explain such repugnant and absurd crimes as the one in Barbados.

For more than 100 years, the shooting of the medical students in 1871 has been recalled and condemned with inextinguishable indignation. For thousands of years, our people will recall, condemn, and abhor this horrible assassination in their deepest souls.

Our athletes sacrificed in the flower of their life and intelligence will be eternal champions in our hearts; their gold medals will not lie on the ocean floor but will rise like unblemished suns and symbols in the Cuban firmament; they will not win the honour of the Olympics, but they have ascended for all time to the beautiful Olympus of martyrs of the homeland!

Our crew members, heroic aviation workers, and selfless compatriots sacrificed under cowardly circumstances that day will live eternally in the memory, affection, and admiration of the people! A homeland ever more revolutionary, more worthy, more socialist, and more internationalist will be the grandiose monument our people will erect to their memory and that of all those who have died or will die for the Revolution!

To our Guyanese and Korean brothers immolated that day goes our most fervent thoughts at this time also. They remind us that imperialism's crimes have no borders, that we all belong to the same human family, and that our struggle is universal.

We cannot say that the sorrow is shared. The sorrow is multiplied. Millions of Cubans shed their tears today together with the dear ones of the victims of the abominable crime. And when an energetic and forceful people cry, injustice trembles!

Even if the USSR Were to Disappear, We Would Continue to Resist

Speech delivered at the commemorative event for the 36th anniversary of the attack on the Moncada Barracks, held in Mayor General 'Ignacio Agramonte' Square, Camagüey, on 26 July 1989, during the 31st Year of the Revolution.

I THOUGHT THAT it might rain during the ceremony. I thought this when I heard that a cold front was moving from east to west. However, after so many months of drought, even if it rains on a day like today, the rain would be welcome.

We do not know if this drizzle will continue all afternoon. We do not know if it will rain harder or if it will stop, but it is up to you to decide if I should hurry, whether I should speak fast, or speak at my usual measured pace. I know that no amount of rain can douse our enthusiasm or dilute our will.

Now, what stands out about this 26 July? I personally, and many visitors to Camaguëy, are impressed by the level of enthusiasm, and fighting spirit found here in this city and this province. Why, after so many years of Revolution, and quite a few have passed, is enthusiasm growing instead of declining? The fighting spirit is growing. How can we explain this? I do not think there is a mystery in this. It is what the Revolution has done for the people. It is what the Revolution has done for mankind throughout the country and in this province. It is what it has meant to our nation and our compatriots to have the opportunity to build their own path and write their own history.

We live in a time of great economic problems throughout the world, above all in the Third World, a time of great economic crises for that world. We are living through a special moment within the world revolutionary movement. We will not sugarcoat the truth. We have to call things the way we see them.

There are difficulties in the world revolutionary movement. There are difficulties in the socialist movements. We cannot even say with confidence that the supplies that have arrived from the socialist camp with clock-like punctuality for the past thirty years will continue to arrive with the same dependability and clock-like punctuality.

The country has been doing more with less than ever, and these projects demonstrate this. These projects were built with less income than ever before. It is possible, that in the future, we will have to continue to work and make an effort and create miracles as a result of the problems we have in receiving supplies from the socialist countries.

Perhaps the greatest problem is the euphoria of imperialism, the empire's triumphalism, and that of the empire's administration.

Never has any administration, not even Reagan's, maintained such cockiness. No other administration has ever sounded so cocky.

Because of the difficulties that are occurring in the socialist camp, especially in certain socialist countries, the Bush administration has given speeches during the past few months, which are based on the premise that the socialist community is nearing its end, that socialism is nearing its end, that socialism will end up in the garbage can of history, which is the place that the brilliant and genius strategists and creators of the socialist movement reserved precisely for capitalism.

Because of the difficulties that are evident and that everyone is aware of, which have existed and still exist in Poland; because of the difficulties of socialism, which have existed and still exist in Hungary; Bush organized a triumphant tour, a triumphant trip to these two countries in recent weeks. It is true that there are difficulties there. He did not go in vain to those countries. He went to encourage capitalist trends that have developed there and to encourage the political problems that have arisen there. Someday it will be the job of historians and scholars to delve deeply into the causes of those problems. I have my ideas about this. However, this is not the time to talk about them.

The fact of the matter is that they have difficulties. In recent elections, the liberal opposition, the pro-capitalist opposition, or, at least, the antisocialist opposition, which has not yet well defined what its intentions are, won almost 100 per cent of the senatorial posts. Today, in Poland, even the leader of that opposition, Mr Walesa, according to the press in our country, told the government of President Jaruzelski, who won the Presidency by one more vote than the minimum required, that the best thing to do would be to have the government turned over to the opposition. In recent days, he has even said that he does not oppose some members of the antisocialist opposition being in the government; however, that they could not count on their support. Walesa said that the only thing the opposition would accept would be for the government to be turned over to them.

The same thing is occurring in Hungary. One day ago, four delegate posts were up for elections, and three of them were overwhelmingly won by the opposition.

What phenomena are we facing? Is this a peaceful transition from socialism to capitalism? It is possible. However, we Cubans do not question it. We defend the sacred right to the independence of each country and each party. This is what we ask for the people of the world. That is what we ask for all the people of Latin America and of the Third World. We ask for the right of each country to build, if it so desires, socialism, which the United States tries very hard to prevent through armed intervention. No one gave us the right to build socialism. We earned it. We conquered it. We defend it.

I think many errors have been made, which have led to these

problems. At times, I even wonder if it would not be better for those new generations that were born under socialism in Poland and in Hungary to take a little trip to capitalism so that they can find out how egoistic, brutal, and dehumanizing a capitalist society is. This is a delicate matter, but these are our most sincere thoughts about these problems.

During Bush's triumphant trip to Gdansk, a city in Poland, according to cables of the most renowned U.S. press agencies, he was received by large crowds carrying banners. I cannot confirm if there were many or a few because I was not there, nor did I see it on television. I read it in the cables. It was reported that many banners read: The Best Communist is a Dead Communist. Notice, those are the feelings of a fascist! The banners, which welcomed Bush in that Polish city, were completely fascist. Naturally, there are two kinds of communists: those who let themselves get killed easily and communists who do not let ourselves get killed easily!

It was with joy that cables of the imperialist news agencies reported that other banners read: Lenin, Jaruzelski, Assassins. I will not defend Jaruzelski. I think he can defend himself. However, what does this mean coming from a city of a country whose freedom cost the lives of one and a half million Soviet soldiers? I am even setting aside the errors in international policy that, at other times, the Soviet Union could have made regarding Poland. I simply reiterate the real fact that one and half million Soviets died fighting next to the Polish people for the freedom of Poland, and now Lenin is called an assassin, the founder of the first socialist state. He made the first great opening for the people of the world. He was the founder of the first socialist state, whose revolution made possible the disappearance of colonialism. Over 100 states have attained independence; over 100 former colonies have attained independence. How repugnant it is to call Lenin an assassin whose people achieved victory against fascism with the sacrifice of twenty-two million deaths among its best children. This is truly bitter.

However, this increases Mr Bush's euphoria. It increases his false pride. It increases the imperialist hostility against Cuba a lot. If Mr Bush bases himself on the premise that socialism is in its decline and that the socialist community is going to disintegrate, what does he think regarding Cuba, this strong, courageous, and heroic Cuba? This is a Cuba that does not surrender or sell itself. If one bases policy on that premise, why change the policy toward Cuba? He is carrying out a peace policy with the great powers and is waging war against the progressive peoples. He is carrying out the policy based on the premise that if socialism ever disintegrates, Cuba would not be able to resist; the Cuban Revolution would disappear. That reasoning increases the aggressive spirit and the hostility of Yankee imperialism against our people, Revolution, and fatherland. These are truths. That is why, today, the empire appears more insolent, wicked, and threatening than ever before.

Just imagine what would happen in the world if the socialist community disappeared? According to that hypothesis, if that was possible, which I do not think it is, the imperialist powers would throw themselves like beasts over the Third World. They would once again distribute the world among themselves, as in the worst of times, before the first proletarian revolution. They would distribute among themselves the oil, natural resources, and the human resources of billions of people in the world. They would once again turn three-quarters of humanity into colonies. However, not even, under those circumstances, would the struggle cease. The peoples would never accept it; the peoples would continue fighting, perhaps now more than ever, and our people, our fatherland, our Revolution would be in the first row of that fight.

Naturally, imperialism has deluded itself, and Bush has deluded himself because of the difficulties that are being experienced by the Soviet Union, the fundamental bulwark of the socialist community. It is true that the USSR is facing difficulties. It is not a secret to anyone, and the dream of the imperialists is that the

USSR will disintegrate. There are difficulties, and they are growing. There are tensions among the nationalities within the USSR.

There are tensions and conflicts. The internal tensions are evident within the USSR, and we have witnessed the strike of hundreds of millions, hundreds of thousands of miners, of strikers in Siberia, Don, and other places. That kind of news fills world reactionaries with joy. That kind of news fills the empire with joy.

We recently received a very warm, very fraternal message from the USSR in the name of the Soviet party, the government, and the state. Our feelings of friendship with the Soviet people and our recognition of the role of that great country are enormous. You know that. Our appreciation of that country is also enormous. Our most fervent desire is that the Soviets will overcome their difficulties, rebuild their unity, and maintain and elevate the great role that the country has played in the world.

The problems in the USSR greatly concern all Third World countries, the old colonies, those peoples who do not want to be colonized again because the USSR was their fundamental and most firm ally. Upon seeing these problems, the imperialist circles dream of an empire lasting 1,000 years, as Adolf Hitler dreamed that his Third Reich would last 1,000 years; but it lasted a very short time.

It is possible that the most reactionary imperialist circles are having these dreams again. I am sure that these dreams will not last very long. This is not a matter of nuclear arms or missiles on one side or the other, or a matter of nuclear disarmament accords, which make us very happy. However, the independence of our people depends on us. It is not dependent upon nuclear weapons from the Soviet Union or from anyone else.

I remember the October crisis and a saying that appeared then: We do not have strategic weapons, but we have moral weapons. Those are the arms with which the peoples defend themselves.

I know their capabilities. I know our people's capabilities, and here today, we are reasoning things out very dispassionately, as one has to reason with the people. On a day like today, at a historic moment like the one that the world is experiencing today, we have to think; we have to reason.

Are we, by any chance, going to put a halt to our progress? Are we going to halt this colossal effort? No, never. Are we going to close our eyes to reality? Are we going to bury our heads in the sand like ostriches in the face of reality? No never. We need to be more realistic than ever, but we have to speak out. We must warn the imperialists so that they do not create any illusions about our Revolution and about the idea that our Revolution will not be able to resist a debate within the socialist community.

If we were to wake up tomorrow or any other day to the news that there had been a large-scale civil war in the USSR, and even if we were to wake up and learn that the USSR had disintegrated, something that we hope never happens, even under those circumstances, Cuba and the Cuban Revolution would continue fighting and resisting. Cuba and the Cuban Revolution would resist. I say this knowingly. I say this calmly and serenely. It is time to speak clearly to the imperialists and to the entire world.

We are not joking. What can frighten us if twenty-seven or twenty-eight years ago we experienced the October crisis? Historians are compiling papers and giving their versions. We have not yet provided our version.

One thing is obvious. We lived through those times, and I do not remember seeing a single Cuban hesitate. The Cubans refused to make any concessions to imperialism; and the Cubans of that generation, many of whom are still living and who have been joined by new generations that are well trained and that have great political awareness, were prepared to die without hesitation, to die rather than retreat, to die rather than give up.

What can frighten our revolutionary people? Nothing in the world can frighten our revolutionary people or cause them to hesitate. A long time ago, a little more than eight years ago, Mr Reagan spouted great threats against Cuba. We have put aside all the little academic books on war. We do lean on all positive experiences, all the experiences in conventional war, and we have adopted the doctrine of the defense of the country and the concept of a war involving all the people. Everyone knows what that concept is, and everyone shares that concept.

It is the philosophy of what our country will do under any circumstances, of what it will do in the event of a total blockade when not even a litre of fuel or a morsel of food can enter the country. What would we do then? We know very well what we would do, and we know we can resist. In the event of war or of being worn out, we know what we would do, and we know how we would resist. In the event of invasion or occupation of the country by Yankee troops, we know how we could resist, how we could fight, and what we would do. We know that sooner or later, the price would be so high for the aggressors that they would have to leave our country, sooner or later.

As for our defense, we learned a long time ago how to count only on our own strength. We know that in the event of a total blockade when not even a litre of fuel or a morsel of food or even one bullet could enter the country, the USSR would not have the conventional forces to break that blockade thousands of miles from its borders. No country can trust its defense to another country. A country can only trust its defense to itself.

Therefore, our minds, our ideas, our concepts are prepared and developed. Do you think we are losing sleep? Do you think we are filled with uncertainty over all these scenarios, these hypothetical situations? Let the imperialists clear the cobwebs from their minds. We know who we are, what we have, what we can do; we know what we can count on.

Therefore, we are at ease. Not even the worst scenario, the worst hypothesis scares us. Since we live in this world and on this planet, we must be aware of the realities, and we must think over the realities. There will be threats in the future as a result of this imperialist policy, these beliefs, this idea that socialism is declining, and that the time is right to exact from Cuba the price of more than thirty years of Revolution. No price will be exacted here.

This is nothing new. This has been going on for a long time. Antonio Maceo already said what would happen to anyone who tried to take over Cuba. This is the people, this is the country, and this is the people of Carlos Manuel de Cespedes and of Jose Marti. This is the country, the same country, the same people of Ignacio Agramonte and Maximo Gomez. This is the same country and the same people of the bronze titan, Antonio Maceo. This is the same country and the same people of Yara and of Bayamo, of the protest from Baragua. This is the same country and the same people. From the Moncada Barracks to internationalism, we all now have a greater revolutionary awareness than ever before in our history. This people and this country will know how to be consistent with their glorious history!

Our Greatest Internationalist Mission is to Save Socialism in Cuba

Speech marking the 30th anniversary of the Committees for the Defense of the Revolution (CDR), held at the 'Karl Marx' theatre, on 28 September 1990, during the 32nd Year of the Revolution.

TODAY IS A truly historic date, and we commemorate it at a truly historic time. It is good that we meet here; that we do not invest a lot of resources, that we do not spend fuel, that we make our presence evident, and that we can communicate from here with all the CDR members in the country.

We have talked about the beautiful history of the Committees for the Defense of the Revolution. The day the idea came about for the original and revolutionary people's movement, which has provided the country with so many services, is remembered here. This movement has served the country in many areas, not only in the struggle against the enemy, but also in the fight against counter-revolution. We have worked for thirty years on this task to defend a Revolution that will soon be thirty-two years old.

We have gone through difficult times, the early years, the fight against bandits, the Bay of Pigs, and later the October crisis, which will also be marked in a few days. There has been a lot of talk about the October crisis lately.

Two or three days ago, I read international dispatches that reported about excerpts of an alleged autobiography or notes written by Khrushchev that has been published in the United States and refer to the October crisis. I am said to have advised

Khrushchev to launch a preventive attack with nuclear missiles against the United States. Perhaps, Khrushchev interpreted some of my messages in this way. However, this was really not the case, and I am not going to explain it now either; fortunately, I have kept the messages I exchanged with Khrushchev during the most challenging hours of the crisis and subsequent days. I have kept them; I thought perhaps they could be saved for posterity. However, since so many indiscretions have been made and so many papers have been published, perhaps I will need to publish them, so those messages are known and my points of view on this matter during the October crisis are known. I will have to do this without waiting too long so that the current generations know well what Cuba's position was at the time.

Perhaps this is done as an instigation; as usual, they have found ways to create animosity and hatred against Cuba within public opinion in the United States. Things are not the way they are said to be. But I maintain the stand that I made then, and I would say in the same way what I said then—I neither regret in the least what I did nor what I said. In the midst of so much gossip and so many people who talk, it would be good to make public some of those messages.

See how the October crisis persists; it was a period that our people endured. It was an extremely challenging time that our people experienced in an extraordinarily cool-headed way and with equanimity.

We have experienced all kinds of threats throughout the years. We have conducted extraordinary internationalist missions, which will remain forever as historic evidence of our people's revolutionary and solidaristic spirit.

So, for us, the revolutionaries, the early ones, I do not want to say the older ones because who considers himself old here? Here, we have old and new CDR members, such as the young lady we handed over the identification cards to; we have all lived through some very interesting experiences. The older ones have experienced them since the Moncada attack and even before. I just handed over a medal to a comrade CDR member, and he was the same CDR member who took me . . . who drove the car in which I travelled before 26 July from Havana to Santiago.

We learned about adversity; we learned about prisons; we learned about exile; we learned about expeditions; we learned about misfortune; and we learned about practically everything throughout these years. Never did pessimism invade our spirit. There was no discouragement in any of those periods. It is very good; it is very good to remember this because those qualities are required from all of us again. When one wants to overcome, when there is the will to overcome, one overcomes. There are no obstacles, and no difficulties can stand in the way of the unwavering will of men and countries.

This is not new. Our people gave extraordinary proof of that spirit long before our independence; our people showed this spirit by fighting for over ten years in the fields of Cuba against one of the most powerful armies of those times. They spent ten years without shoes; they spent ten years living off the land; and after those ten years, the immortal symbol of Baragua emerged. After some of the people's fighters got tired, they gave what truly represented the spirit of our people, and they planted it there eternally. That is why the Cubans returned to the struggle, and that is why we one day reached complete independence—an independence that today is greater than ever. Even those who sometimes called us satellites, even those who wanted us to obey orders from abroad, and those who, so many times, tried to humiliate us with those strange words did not offend us because solidarity is a principle for us. To be a brother-of-revolutionaries is a principle; it always has been and always will be so. I hope that those who, at one time, thought we were satellites no longer have the remotest shadow of doubt that we were not, we are not, and will never be anybody's satellite.

We should say that we built this Revolution ourselves—no one built it for us, no one defended it for us, no one saved it for us—we did it ourselves; we defended it ourselves; we saved it ourselves; and, we will continue to do so. We will continue to defend it and continue to save it as often as necessary. We did not ask anyone for permission to build the Revolution, and we did not count on anyone else. International solidarity emerged; economic cooperation and cooperation-in-arms arose; it was magnificent, beautiful, and we will always appreciate this.

However, not long ago, there was talk of the explosion of the *La Coubre* ship in 1960. It was obviously an act of sabotage prepared by the enemy. It was set up to explode when the ship was being unloaded in our docks. It cost the lives of about one hundred workers and soldiers.

Well, at that time, we had not received a single weapon from anyone, and we were buying them with our scarce resources. We distributed them throughout the mountains, and we prepared—alone, by ourselves, on our own account, and with our own weapons—our guerrilla war against the imperialist invader, which began with their threats. When we established our agrarian reform and the first revolutionary laws, we did not even have economic or political relations with the USSR. We did this ourselves and on our own!

Nevertheless, the existence of the October Revolution was a privilege, as we have said many times. The glorious and thousands-of-times glorious October Revolution was a fortunate thing, an extraordinary event for our Revolution and our country.

Today, when some people even want to smash Lenin statues to pieces, we see how Lenin's image grows and looms larger in our hearts and thoughts. Lenin and his thought meant and still means a lot to those of us who have interpreted his thought, along with the thoughts of Marx and other revolution's theorists, in the way that they should be interpreted—in an original manner—by each country and each revolutionary process. That thought maintains all its validity in our revolutionary process at a time when some people abhor the idea of calling themselves Communists. There are people like this throughout the world in industrial quantities. They do not want to call themselves Communists. They call themselves socialists, social-democrats, social-whatever, and social-nothings.

Lenin's work will last throughout history; he helped to change the world. Lenin's work led to the emergence of the first socialist state in the history of humanity; that state saved humanity from fascism. Without the sacrifice of Soviet lives, fascism would have been imposed upon the world for at least a brief period of time; everyone would have personally learned of the horrors of fascism.

That first socialist state meant the development of the people's liberation movement and the end of colonialism. When the imperialists wanted to destroy the Revolution, when the imperialists blockaded us and tried to strangle us with hunger—the existence of the Soviet Union, of the Socialist bloc—meant a lot to us; it was something of extraordinary value to our country under those circumstances.

Naturally, political and economic relations were established and evolved into truly admirable methods of cooperation, into new forms of relations that meant the end of unequal trade, which meant applying the best elements of Marxist-Leninist principles.

In the first years and over the course of time, economic agreements were established between socialist countries and Cuba and between the Soviet Union and Cuba. When, in practice, we discovered the phenomenon of unequal trade with the Soviet Union. In practice, we discovered that the prices of products we imported were constantly rising while the prices of our products remained the same for a five-year period. This led us to establish a new correlation of prices between what we exported and imported. As the prices rose on the merchandise we imported, the prices of our own products rose. There was never anything fairer than this in the history of economic relations between peoples—between industrialized countries and underdeveloped countries that were colonies and that were exploited and kept underdeveloped for centuries of colonialism or neo-colonialism. Over the years, a basis was established for trade between socialist countries and Cuba, between the USSR and Cuba, which has lasted for many years.

We have been developing our country on those bases. Economic and social development has been formed on those bases, which were very fair, solid, and spanned many years; they remained until our development levels were similar to those countries' industrial development levels. That historic period has not concluded; only a part of that historic period has ended; only a part of that historic phase has passed. Our industries were created on those bases; our agriculture was developed and mechanized on those bases; electricity was established throughout the country on those bases.

At the triumph of the Revolution in 1959, only 50 per cent of the population had access to electricity; there was a population of 6.5 million people, only 3.2 million people had access to electricity. Now, 92 per cent of our population has access to electricity; over 9.5 million people have access to electricity. This is three times the number of people who had access to electricity at the time of the triumph of the Revolution. Today, electricity reaches the most isolated corners of the country; it has been taken into the mountains, everywhere; electricity brings a radical change in the way of life.

As our population notably increased its per capita income, not only did the number of people with access to electricity increase, the per capita consumption of electricity also considerably increased. This made it possible for millions of people to access all kinds of domestic electrical appliances such as television sets, radios, electric irons, fans, mixers, as many domestic electrical appliances as you can mention.

The five-year plans between socialist countries and us, and between the Soviet Union and us, were prepared on that basis. Plans for fifteen and twenty years were talked about and prepared on that basis. There was a constant exchange of views between the planning organizations of all those countries and us.

Suddenly, within an extremely brief period, the socialist camp disappeared; it is a euphemism to speak of a socialist camp now. Reference is made to the Council of Mutual Economic Assistance (CMEA); the CMEA is still there; it is there as a formality because it hardly ever meets; to tell you the truth, when it meets, I do not know what is going to be discussed. Some of those with whom we had established very close relations, such as the GDR, have virtually disappeared. On 3 October, that is, in five or six days, it will be part of a unified Germany. In other countries, they are trying to build capitalism quickly.

So, the country lost those pillars represented by agreements with countries from the socialist camp. Other socialist countries are still struggling to maintain as much as possible the social achievements in the middle of very great difficulties, because all these problems affect them.

The USSR is left; when I mention the Eastern European countries, I do not mention the USSR because it is in a different category. The USSR is going through a deep political, economic, and social crisis; this is nothing new; we all know about it because of the news that we see in the press. The USSR, of all the pillars, was the strongest pillar of our economic and social development. We are building a nuclear power plant with the USSR; it was going to have four 400,000-kilowatt reactors, the construction of two of them is at an advanced stage. How much we could use those reactors now! Those reactors have not fallen behind schedule through our fault. When will they be ready? We do not know. Will they ever be completed? We do not even know that. We built a large nickel production plant with the USSR; we are building another similar nickel plant in Camarioca with the USSR and other socialist countries. We built large thermoelectric power plants with the USSR, and we built the first phase of the oil refinery with the USSR; all this has been completed.

The investment is enormous; I should mention that the country has invested around a billion pesos in the Moa plant, which is now at a standstill due to a lack of fuel. Tens of thousands of tonnes of equipment has been installed; thousands and thousands of homes have been built; an ultramodern hospital is being built, which is almost complete; we have built roads there—everything to develop the nickel industry in that region.

The refinery, the first phase, was being finished; it was supposed to be able to refine 3 million barrels of oil, and now we cannot even make it run.

We have the work of more than 10,000 men, done over many years, invested in the electronuclear plant, and its fate is now uncertain.

That is why we should be very familiar with things, very familiar with how things are. Does the USSR or the Government of the USSR want to hurt us like this? No. The USSR does not want to hurt us like this.

This year, we have a deficit of 2 million tonnes of fuel supplies, and there are a lot of raw materials, which would be too many to list and which are very important, such as industrial raw materials, where significant supply deficits exist. These raw materials have been agreed upon, contracts were established regarding them. These materials affect the economy in such areas as fertilizers and many other things.

Did the USSR want to harm us like this? No. The Soviet Government has made every effort, and I say this with all honesty, to fulfil the supplies we agreed upon. They have wanted to fulfil these goals; the USSR says that they have made a great effort to do so; they have met their commitments regarding certain items. We have received some machinery, machinery that will now have to be studied. What machinery do we really need? It depends on the availability of fuel. We have continued to receive important products because the USSR has made a great effort. We know it, and it is fair to say so.

This has nothing to do with the Yankee position. The Yankees beg the USSR, implore it, tell it, and practically demand, publicly demand and they do not hide it, to end economic cooperation with Cuba as a condition to continue improving relations between the USSR and the United States, as a condition for the USSR to receive economic aid from the United States during its difficult times. The United States demands that the USSR end the kind of economic relations it has with Cuba, end what they call aid, and end what is the result of a fair exchange between the two countries. They require this, demand it. They make it a condition. It is an embarrassment. We have been able to observe to what extremes the imperialists have gone. It has asked the USSR to please help destroy the Cuban Revolution. It has invited the USSR to join the US blockade against Cuba and end relations between the socialist camp and Cuba and between the USSR and Cuba. Yet that blockade still exists, and it is more rigorous and merciless than ever, against our country. Now the United States, which has not been able to beat us, which has not been able to defeat us, is asking the USSR to join the US blockade against Cuba.

That is not what the government of the Soviet Union thinks; that is not what the Soviet leaders think. However, some people in the USSR are delighted with the idea; some people in the USSR think that this is the perfect time to curry favour with the empire and end the bases of economic relations between the USSR and Cuba. Some people think this way, and not only do they think it, but some of them have expressed this to the Yankees. They have expressed this to Yankee officials; they have given themselves the responsibility of saying this everywhere. We learn of these things because we are not stupid, deaf, maimed, or blind. And of course, we always receive the news. Some of them have said this, and they have not only said it to the Yankees; they have said it to others. We know this.

However, that is not the Soviet government's way of thinking. Even amid its problems and difficulties, it has made great efforts to meet its commitments to our country. Nevertheless, today, we do not know what the basis of our trade with the USSR will be next year. No one knows currently how much they are going to pay for our sugar, for our products. What price are we going to be charged for the products supplied by the USSR? What amount of fuel are we going to receive? No one knows this at this time, although practically only three months remain before the end of the year.

In the past, we would have five-year plans that were drafted over a period of time. Agreements were reached almost a year ahead of time, a great time in advance. Normally, we would have reached agreements for almost all the merchandise at this point in the year, but very few agreements have been reached right now. We know nothing at this time, and we are only three months away from 1991.

Of course, fuel is one of the most sensitive areas because the Persian Gulf crisis aggravates this situation. This crisis has been a tragedy for the world, but particularly for Cuba, because the price of oil, which had been 14 pesos a barrel before the crisis, today is approximately 40 pesos. Imagine if we are asked to pay this crisis price for oil while being expected to receive the garbage-dump price for sugar, the 'price' on the world market, which does not exist anywhere. In the economic relations between the East European Community and the countries from which it buys sugar, the price is not the so-called world market price even when they have a sugar surplus.

Just imagine what the union of those two factors means: the crisis in the USSR and crisis in the Gulf. Where can we find a tonne of oil under those conditions, and at what price? And when oil prices spiral upward outrageously, this always works to the detriment of the prices of the essential products of the Third World countries. It produces a reduction in the prices of the other products because those high oil prices cause a recession. There is a reduction in the demand for the other products. The governments do not have enough money even to operate. The countries have no resources; they must devote almost all their resources to oil; consequently, they have much fewer resources to buy other products.

You can see that 2 tonnes of sugar would be required to buy a tonne of oil at those prices. You know how much is invested in producing a tonne of sugar, starting with planting the sugarcane. The soil is prepared, the sugarcane is planted, cleaned, and cut, then the sugar is produced and shipped. Based on those agreements and our relations with the USSR, our country had reached a consumption level of

13 million tonnes. Imagine having sugar at the world market price and oil at the world market price—this special price, because oil does not just have a crisis price—it has privileged prices, it has monopoly prices. Cuba would need 26 million tonne of sugar,

26 million, just to purchase the 13 million tonne of fuel that the country would need. In other words, almost all the sugar that is sold in the world or even more than what is sold. Because, while oil had increased in price considerably in the 1970s because of one of those crises in the Middle East, one of those wars, reaching a price of twenty, twenty-five, and even thirty dollars a tonne; with incalculable disruption to the world, it had recently begun to decline in price. But while oil had increased to fifteen times its price, it's now twenty times its traditional price; sugar is at its usual price. In other words, in comparing sugar and oil today, we would have one at its usual garbage-dump price, compared with a monopolistic crisis price that is twenty times greater than the usual price for oil.

We have been selling sugar to the USSR at a price that is more or less equivalent to the production cost of a tonne of sugar in the USSR, at times for even less than the production cost of a tonne of sugar in the USSR. As a matter of fact, the price that we have paid for oil in recent years is much higher than the production cost of a tonne of oil. Actually, oil is one of the world's most privileged products, with an inflated price that is many times the cost of production.

Therefore, this is the kind of problem that we are facing, without being at all at fault. After all, we have made enormous efforts to find fuel. You know about the billions of metres that we have drilled in search of fuel throughout the years, with the cooperation of the USSR. We have built causeways; we have done everything; we have only been able to increase our oil production by a little over a million tonne of oil. We have made a great effort, with Soviet cooperation, to build that nuclear energy plant; it is actually far behind schedule because of factors beyond our control.

This is the kind of difficulty that the country and the Revolution are facing today. I wish to say that the current limitations can become greater. I am speaking to you with great clarity. I ask you today, on this 28 October, on this thirtieth anniversary: What are we going to do? Give up? Never. What are we going to do? What are we going to do? Are we going to renounce the Revolution? Renounce socialism? Renounce independence? Never. What we have to do is resist and fight. We must resist, fight, and win, of course.

Well, are we worse off than our ancestors were in the ten-year war of independence? Absolutely not! Are we going to be in a worse situation than we would be in the event of a total military blockade of the country?

In fact, in our defense plans in the last few years, we have worked out all the ideas of what we should do in the event of a total air and naval blockade against our country. Well, circumstances resembling a total blockade of the country could arrive at any moment. But it would never be the same. Our ships would travel, taking away our products and bringing what we may have been able to purchase. We could trade with many countries, and the conditions would not be similar to a total blockade. We have said, we have asserted, and we believe that we are ready to endure a total blockade of the country and ensure the life of the country even under those conditions and ensure the defense of the country under those conditions.

So, the elements, adverse circumstances—the combination of all the factors I explained before—could lead us to challenging and harsh trials. And this is the hope of the imperialists. Today, their greatest hope is that our situation will become so difficult because of the situation in Eastern Europe and the USSR that we will not be able to endure. That is their hope, the hope of the counter-revolutionary community in Miami; those rats who have their suitcases packed and all that kind of thing, and there are surveys and studies on what to do and what they will do, already thinking about the post-revolutionary period.

It has been very useful to have these programs and plans for the special period, because the special period was thought up in case of a war, in case of a total blockade of the country in which nothing could get in or out. The special period we are talking about now has emerged as a concept in facing the problems that I have mentioned, the problems in Eastern Europe and the USSR. The concept of the special period in peacetime has emerged. And we are undoubtedly already entering this special period in peacetime. And it is inevitable that we will fall into this special period in all its harshness in peacetime. We will have to undergo this trial.

We have already had to take the initial measures in electricity consumption. We have already taken other measures. We had been taking them for months in the hope that the shortfalls could be resolved. But we had already been reducing fuel consumption until we reached a point at which it was impossible not to take more radical measures, such as the ones that have been taken in industry, transportation, those taken with electricity, etc.

Now new measures have been taken concerning the distribution of products, and situations will inevitably arise that are impossible to predict at this time, impossible to predict. What will the situation be like in 1991? What is to come? What raw materials will we have? How much fuel? Under what conditions? We cannot give figures. We must be prepared to work with less and less and less and less and almost with nothing. Well, that would be an extreme situation, that would be an extreme situation, but we must think about these alternatives, which could be the most critical thing. So, there would be various measures we would have to take under these conditions.

What are we trying to do, and what are we doing, given this situation? We propose that if we have to face a special period in peacetime, a harsh period, our task should be not only to survive but to develop.

We must be prepared. However, *compañeras* and *compañeros*, there is something I want you to keep in mind. Only a socialist system can face this. In a capitalist system having these kinds of problems, they would double or triple the prices, and that would be it. The poorer people with less income would have no electricity, and that would be it. Only a socialist system faces the problems in the way we are doing. A capitalist system would even go as far as to ration electricity and solve the problem with price increases. What if we were to raise the price to 20 or 25 cents a kilowatt? You can be sure that we would save many more kilowatts. However, who would be penalized; who would be affected? Who would be harmed? The workers, the poorer people, would be harmed. Those poor sectors would be affected the most.

What would a capitalist system do in the case of an energy crisis? It could do nothing. It would have no way out. Prices would increase, and some people would resort to stealing electricity from their neighbours. In a capitalist system, generally speaking, no one is allowed to do this, but the prices would increase anyway. They would raise the price to fifty and reduce the number of trips from twenty-six thousand to eight thousand. Two-thirds of the fifteen thousand Havana city bus employees would be fired. Two-thirds are a lot, and we would have a conflict.

However, what do the capitalists do? What are many Latin American countries doing every day? They have never had a crisis like the one that is coming because of fuel. They fire millions of people, increase prices, and crush the people; and the capitalists are only a privileged or super-privileged minority.

Over the last few years, we have seen in Latin America the famous shock measures that the World Bank and the IMF are recommending to the formerly socialist Eastern Bloc countries, those that decided to build capitalism. The World Bank and the IMF advise them to throw millions of people into the streets and increase prices. That is how capitalists solve the problem.

However, the Revolution will face this time without sending anyone into the street, without depriving a single citizen of his resources, and without leaving anyone unemployed. Money may be plentiful; I will not deny it; however, one of the problems we will face is that we cannot expect to have new electric home appliances because many consumer goods will decrease logically. This is regrettable, but it is better than not having food or medicine.

Not a single citizen will be deserted, and that is a characteristic of our socialism. Not a single citizen will be abandoned. We challenge capitalism to solve the problem in this manner and to face difficulties such as these in this manner.

It is possible that the situation with the fuel and raw materials will force us to reduce the workweek. Many similar measures are already being taken. Some people work an extra hour so that they do not have to work on Saturday. Some other people are working double shifts every other day.

We are searching for many formulas, but we do not want to sacrifice the citizen. At the most, the worker will earn free time, but he will not be on the streets without a job. This is the real humane way.

Imperialists talk so much about human rights, but their formulas are cruel and always at the workers' or people's expense. Humane treatment may be the great virtue of our system when it faces problems such as this one. If we had a capitalist system in our country, this would be absolutely impossible. The situation would explode. There would be ten revolutions. Some countries are facing a similar situation now.

We have experienced oil crises in the past, but we did not have a crisis in the socialist world. Now, we are facing two crises simultaneously; the crisis in the socialist world and the oil crisis, which has resulted from the Persian Gulf conflict. Both are very serious problems. Our other problems have combined with this new problem, but the situation is disastrous for other countries. With oil prices at forty dollars per barrel, no one knows what will happen to over a hundred countries in the world. No one knows what will happen in those countries. But this is not all.

We will come together to face that situation. We will bear the burden of this problem together. We will work together to save the country. We will conduct activities that will allow us to find definitive solutions in the future, but we always work as we should work under these circumstances. We have to think that we will attain our total economic independence at any price one day, our total economic independence. And we will attain it; life will have us face that challenge; and we will mature and will be stronger and more prepared. How are we going to attain that goal? Although ours is a small country that does not produce important hydrocarbons, we have this. We have our people's intelligence. We have our intelligence, the intelligence that has developed the Revolutionthroughout these years. We have developed abilities. We have these two things.

Our moral values and revolutionary principles helped us send over 300,000 internationalist combatants. No other country in the world has done that. Those values must be present now. This country is now required to express its internationalism; it is required to conduct an extraordinary internationalist mission: to save the Cuban Revolution—to save socialism in Cuba!

That will be the greatest internationalist service that our people may ever offer humanity. Revolutionary ideas are not defeated; they are going through hard times, and they will return. The more injustice there is in the world, the faster they will return. The more exploitation there is in the world, the more hunger there is, the more chaos there is in the world, the faster the revolutionary ideas will return.

We, who are the standard-bearers of these ideas, must uphold them. History has given us this mission. As I said, we have the intelligence, moral virtue, courage, and heroism to carry out that mission.

You may have heard at the United Nations the gratitude shown for our representation at the Security Council regarding the Persian Gulf crisis. We conducted ourselves with absolute dignity and with a total spirit of justice. We have made this extraordinary effort for peace, to find a solution without war, but a fair solution.

We did not hesitate in rejecting and condemning Kuwait's occupation and annexation. We did this based on the norms and principles of international law, which we believe must prevail in our world. Therefore, we did not hesitate to support the resolutions that condemned those actions, which according to our judgment, violated international law. But at the same time, we have strongly opposed everything we consider unfair. One of the most unfair things is the attempt to defeat a whole nation through starvation. That is what the blockade amounts to!

At first, we struggled to have food and medicine excluded from the blockade because if making innocent people hostages is commendable, which we oppose and always will oppose; it is even more cruel to try to kill millions of men, women, senior citizens, and children by starvation to achieve a determined objective.

The blockade does not only affect the military force but the civilian population too. There are millions of innocent men, women, senior citizens, and children among the civilian population. This is revolting. That is what the United States wants and has demonstrated at the United Nations, in light of Cuba's efforts to define the blockade properly and try to have an exception to food and medicines.

We must first save the homeland, and we want a free and independent homeland, a land that is now more independent than ever. We want always to have a proud and independent homeland instead of a Yankee colony. We must save the homeland; we must save the Revolution; and we must save socialism. This is the task we urge the 7.5 million CDR members to undertake today.

Defeating Neoliberalism Will Allow for Hope in the Future

Speech at the closing of the 4th meeting of the Sao Paulo Forum held at the Palacio de Convenciones, Havana on 24 July 1993, during the 35th Year of the Revolution.

FELLOW MEMBERS OF the Sao Paulo Forum:

I have followed closely and with great attention the entire debate of the first three days on this fundamental topic related to the political and economic situation in Latin America.

I was highly interested in knowing how the Left in Latin America thought at this time, based on the conviction that we are living through the most challenging times in the history of our continent, that we are living through one of the most challenging times in the world, and that we are also experiencing one of the most challenging moments in the history of the Left.

I must confess that I feel astonished and stimulated to have had this opportunity to listen to them; the great community of ideas, criteria, concepts, and concerns among all of us is extraordinarily striking. I am struck by the practically unanimous opinion about what neoliberalism means in Latin America and the Caribbean.

I have felt like someone put into a sauna at 110 degrees and then thrown into cold water at 4 or 5 degrees. Having just returned from the Third Summit Conference of Heads of State and Government of Latin America, this is how I felt.

One of my significant concerns in the summit conferences I have attended has been the triumphant euphoria around neoliberalism; the enormous optimism seen at the three summits: Guadalajara, Madrid, and Salvador de Bahía.

It was in Madrid where most apologies were made for neoliberalism, as though the solution to all problems of Latin America and the world had been found.

In these three summits, I followed comrade Marina, and as a matter of honour, I felt I had to express that I did not share their criteria and conceptions; I respected them but did not share their views. I wanted to save my historical responsibility.

However, at this last summit, there was something new: social problems were discussed for the first time. This came about due to Brazil's position. They raised the issue of development as the summit's central theme, with particular emphasis on social development; they had already talked about the dramatic social situation in Latin America. There was no talk of the Caribbean; the summit meeting was only for Latin American countries.

In my opinion, it was a modest advance. However, the understanding that neoliberalism had discovered poverty as if it were new was striking; and that, of course, neoliberalism is going to solve it by generating wealth.

This reigning euphoria was also expressed by the Group of Seven in Tokyo when they claimed the great success of Latin America was due to some improvements in specific economic indices. For example, there was a reduction in inflation; there was a reduction in the budget deficit; there was a modest 2.4 per cent increase in the Gross Domestic Product, which manifested itself in different proportions: in some countries, it fell; in some others, it rose; and in some countries, it grew more than others; in addition, there had been some capital inflow. The euphoria, the apology, and the great hopes placed on neoliberalism were based upon these elements.

Besides, there were obvious things that everyone was witnessing: the disastrous situation in all areas of today's social life. There have never been more poor people in Latin America; there has never been more unemployment in Latin America; and there has never been greater inequality in Latin America. We could say that there was never more neglect of education, more neglect of health, more neglect of poverty, and more neglect of the homeless. There have never been more homeless children or children living on the streets. There has never been a greater increase in social violence, vices, drug usage, and drug trafficking.

There has never been a greater renunciation of values that were always sacred to us Latin Americans. And it can be said that there was never less hope because neoliberalism is not a theory of development; neoliberalism is the doctrine of the total plunder of our peoples. Neoliberalism does not promise us anything; even in developed and overdeveloped countries, it has not solved socioeconomic issues; they are changing governments because they have not even been able to solve the problem of unemployment.

What would agriculture in the United States be without Latin American immigrants? Who would grow tomatoes, asparagus, fruits, citrus and food, in general, in California and throughout the territory of that country, and even in Canada itself? Who would grow them without the Latin American immigrants? And despite that, the unemployment situation is so desperate that it engenders this type of reaction and criminalization against immigrants. And more and more worrisome crimes are being committed.

The Berlin Wall has fallen, and now they are building a wall that goes from the Baltic to the Mediterranean, while other walls have not been removed, such as the one that separates North Korea and South Korea. And for the one that separates Mexico from the United States, they've run out of electronic equipment to use and measures to keep the Mexicans from crossing in search of jobs or better living conditions in the north.

Before, everyone who crossed from Eastern Europe to Western Europe was greeted with applause and parties, and now they adopt stringent laws. Now that the socialist camp and the Soviet Union have become a third or fourth world, they cannot immigrate from east to west. Migration is becoming one of the greatest tragedies and one of the greatest nightmares of the developed capitalist world. There are hundreds of millions of people, and their number is increasing, who want to emigrate from poverty and despair towards those highly propagandized consumer societies.

The developed capitalist world has not been able to solve its problems. What hope can we, in the Third World, have of solving our problems with these neoliberal recipes?

If we talk about Latin America, with euphoria, it is mentioned that the amount of capital invested in Latin America has increased in the last two years. Yet, this capital is insignificant compared to the 700 billion dollars that Latin America has lost over the past twelve years to only two causes: debt service payments and unequal exchange. This does not include capital flight, which you know is vast.

Neoliberalism has aggravated the phenomenon of unequal exchange; it is eliminating all the protection measures and all the agreements on essential products with which the Third World countries tried to defend themselves. In addition, prices fell extraordinarily; thus, in just ten years between 1982 and 1992, prices have been depressed by 28 per cent. Neoliberalism has come to aggravate this phenomenon.

For a long time, we have been sources of capital for the developed capitalist countries; but never before has the loss of natural resources, which were fiercely defended and made the fundamental basis of the political movements in Latin America, and the loss of public services and their control been so great.

And Europe does not provide a good example. Until recently, the share of public spending in the Gross Domestic Product of European countries was 48 per cent in England, 52 per cent in France, around 47 per cent in Germany, and a slightly lower 33 per cent in Japan. Those countries have tried to preserve essential public services; they have not privatized them, yet we are required to privatize them all. That is the truly tragic phenomenon that we are perceiving.

A part of the capital that Latin American countries have received was the result of the sale of public service companies; it is not capital that the countries have developed. Even a large part of this capital is 'hot money', which is invested in short time financial products for purely speculative purposes.

Is this how we are going to solve the problems of Latin America? It is the region of the world with the most concentrated land ownership, is the region of the world where wealth is distributed the most unequally. Where 40 per cent of the poorest population receives 11 per cent of income, and 20 per cent of the ones with the best economic situation receive almost 60 per cent of the income. Does neoliberalism promise to change that situation?

What is so strange is that Latin America today has 270 million inhabitants living in poverty and 84 million living in extreme poverty? What is so strange is that there are fifty-seven deaths for every one thousand children before their fifth birthday? What is so strange about epidemics spreading, like cholera? What is so strange is that AIDS is multiplying at an accelerated rate, that there are around a million people affected by this disease that was imported, that was not born in Latin America. There are 200,000 women and 10,000 children affected with AIDS? What is so strange is that 36 per cent of kids don't make it to fourth grade? What is so strange is that if in 1964 there were 3.3 beds for every 1,000 inhabitants, now there are 2.05 beds for every 1,000 inhabitants? What reasons do we have to be happy?

This situation can also be seen in the rest of the Third World in similar numbers: 1.2 billion in poverty, 786 million chronically malnourished, 180 million severely malnourished children, 1.5 billion people without medical care, 1 billion people illiterate, and 270 million women between the ages of 19 and 49 years old are anaemic. From whom do we receive that inheritance, if not from colonialism, from neocolonialism? What remedies have they brought to our problems? These populations are living worse today than they did under colonialism, and are these problems that neoliberalism will solve for us?

Another very strong criterion that I was able to appreciate in the summit meetings is an attempt to discredit the state and minimize its role; the idea that the state should only dedicate itself to education, to public health, to any of those activities that contribute to public order; but that any productive activity must exclusively be private activity, because private activity is the only one that can manage it; it is the only one that can be efficient. I felt an obligation to defend the poor state. I imagined that any day, in one of those meetings, almost everyone would be dressed in red and black as a symbol of the disappearance of the state, remembering the best times of anarchism, with all the respect that anarchism deserves; since I respect anarchism more than neoliberalism.

I had to explain some of the things that the state does, and I said: if the state cannot manage a factory, it is difficult for the state to manage a hospital. I explained what the state had done in our country with the hospitals, the health indices that our people had, and how despite the special period, at this moment, infant mortality was at 9.3 per 1,000 live births in Cuba. That means, notwithstanding the very difficult period we are living in, the number of infants dying in the first year of their lives is still less than ten. It was the work of the state; it was the work of the state to train 48,000 doctors, which are those that Cuba has today, and by the end of this year, it will have more than 50,000, despite all those that imperialism took away. At the triumph of the Revolution in 1959—3,000 of the 6,000 doctors we had, left the country. What the state has done in education, the universities that the state has created, the hundreds of thousands of university professionals trained, all of whom are children of workers, peasants, humble people from the countryside.

We can explain the efforts that the state has made in the field of science. Our country has almost 200 science and technology institutions with magnificent scientists. We have developed some vaccines that are unique in the world and techniques for the care of certain diseases which are unique in the world. We have created dozens of products that have come from laboratories, which are state laboratories, and are not from transnational companies who have respect for the progress that our country is making in the field of science. This has been the work of the Revolution; this has been through State institutions.

What is the objective of discrediting the state at all costs and demanding the state's non-participation in the economy? This has nothing to do with other ideas that might be discussed about what the state should do and what the state should not try to do.

In those meetings, I reiterate that a strong feeling is observed against the state, reducing its role to zero. However, I must honestly say that there were some participants who, when I raised some points relating to the state as a matter of principle, as a matter of honour, told me that they agreed with most of the things I had raised in that sense.

These are realities. The social problems of Latin America and the objective difficulties that the people and the masses have are greater than those they ever had after the Second World War; they are greater than those they had in the sixties and seventies. I believe that our hemisphere is experiencing a much more difficult situation than at any other time in history.

Unfortunately, this coincided with the disaster of the socialist camp, with the disappearance of the Soviet Union, with the illusions that many had made for themselves, and with the noble wishes of many people for socialism to be perfected. Nobody could be against the idea that socialism was to be perfected, but socialism was not to be destroyed! Hundreds of millions of people in the world wanted the improvement of socialism and not the destruction of socialism. However, what unfortunately resulted was the destruction of socialism, and even those who said they wanted socialism, and more socialism, and better socialism, today write that socialism was a dream, that socialism is a utopia; unrealizable.

Here in this forum, socialism is not being defended, and no one can pretend that in this forum, socialism is considered as an objective. No one can claim that the conditions, both objective and subjective, at this moment are conducive to the construction of socialism. I think there are other priorities right now. It does not mean that whoever wants to build it does not build it; this does not mean that anyone will be forbidden to build socialism if they can build it. We have been fighting for decades to build socialism and have no regrets about it. We plan to continue building socialism, and we plan to save socialism in our country—and we plan to perfect socialism. But I believe that today in Latin America, the priority battle—in my opinion—is to defeat neoliberalism; because if we do not defeat neoliberalism, we disappear as nations; we disappear as independent states; and we will be more colonialized than countries ever were.

Defeating neoliberalism would be creating hope for the future and preserving conditions to continue advancing. Because capitalism will limit our progress, and there will be no human progress unless we go beyond the borders of capitalism; but that will be the task of others. This will be a task for other moments, not necessarily the task of other generations. I see many young people here among the participants, and I think many of them have the possibility of building socialism in their countries.

I think we have a duty to be politicians; I think we have a duty to be intelligent because if we don't use intelligence, we won't get anywhere. But, at the same time, we have a duty to be serious; we have a duty to defend our principles. And really, under no circumstances can we sacrifice a principle for the sake of a chimera, because today, the future policy of the United States in relation to Latin America is an unknown; it may be a chimera.

But no matter how many good wishes we may have for some

changes, it is difficult to implement them. I believe in the struggle; above all, I believe in the struggle of the peoples; I believe in the struggle of the masses. And recently, in Latin America, we have had important examples of what the people can do without weapons; even look at what the people can do without arms; of what the masses can do, what conscience can do, and what ethics can do. At the same time that these negative phenomena are taking place, there is inevitably greater participation of the peoples in the events.

We must admire the greatness of Bolívar when at such an early time, he raised the idea of a union of the peoples of Latin America; at a time when there was no aviation, no motor vehicles, no locomotives, no telegraph, no telephone, no radio, nor television. Today in a matter of seconds, anyone communicates from Mexico with Buenos Aires; the news is simultaneously broadcasted to all parts of the world; in a matter of hours, thousands and thousands of kilometres are travelled. Today there is fabulous media, and Bolívar was already talking about the need for the union of Latin America when none of that existed; perhaps it was then impossible. Later, Martí was one of the most fervent defenders of the unity of Latin America; eighty years later, already in another era, he raised it as a vital need of our peoples. Almost one hundred and seventy years have passed since independence, and Latin America is still divided; it is balkanized.

He said it is not a sentimental question; it is a vital question; it is a question of survival. We are living in a world of great economic and industrial giants, of great economic and political communities. What prospects for independence, security, and peace would our divided peoples have? What prospects for development and well-being would a divided Latin America have? Of course, it is a challenging task; it is enough to analyze isolated integration efforts to understand how difficult the task of economic integration is; but we need economic integration, political integration, and to overcome all obstacles. It is not the transnationals that will integrate us and those that are going to unite us. When we speak of the economic and political integration of Latin America, we speak, above all, of a question of conscience, of a conscience that must be formed, of a thought that must be created. If you don't create a thought, if you don't develop consciousness, nothing will be possible.

I speak to you with the conviction of the purity of intentions that animates you, of the beautiful ideals that inspire you in the struggle, all of you who wish for a better world, for a better Latin America.

I speak to people whom I admire, and I must admire you when I measure the magnitude of the task before you. I have seen your firm hope even with the future challenges of the next years.

When on the fortieth anniversary we fight for our Revolution and our socialism, we also must think about those who fought before us; we must think of Bolívar, for example, San Martín, Sucre, O'Higgins, Hidalgo, Morelos, Morazán, and Juárez. Was their fight useless? Wouldn't they perhaps be sadder than we are in witnessing this panorama of Latin America?

What would Bolívar say if he were seeing what we see today if he were seeing the emergence of those colossal empires around us, enormous centres of economic and political power? What would he say if he saw what they are doing to us, what they are imposing on us? What would Bolívar say about the foreign debt? What would Bolívar say about neoliberalism?

What would Martí say if he could see everything we see in this America, an America he dreamt of being united one day, for which he gave his life? Because before he died, he said that everything he had done was precisely to strengthen Latin America and prevent the advance of the colossus of the north on the peoples of Latin America?

How many men have fought over so many years! But I think that if they lived now, as we do, they would not be sorry; they would not be discouraged; they would continue to conceive the same dreams as we conceive their dreams and our dreams today. They would not renounce the struggle, as you do not renounce it, as we Cubans do not renounce our struggles.

In one of the speeches, I already told you that we had to know how to distinguish between what we should do to save the homeland, the Revolution, and the conquests of socialism, and what we should do to perfect socialism. And we will know how to fulfil those duties. We will do whatever it takes to save the country, save the Revolution, save the principles of socialism. But what we do, we will do because what we want is to save and not destroy; and if to save, we must destroy, we prefer to be destroyed together with what we have done and what we have created.

Times are challenging, but I can say with absolute conviction that with the courage and intelligence of our people and with your solidarity, which has expressed itself so spontaneously and so generously at this meeting, you'll have in the Cuban people the firmest and most loyal comrades-in-struggle, who will know how to fight, how to fulfil their duty, and how to carry out their purpose of saving the homeland, the Revolution, and the conquests of socialism.

I say conquests because today, we cannot speak of the pure, the ideal, the perfect socialism that we dream of because life forces us to make concessions.

What is this about having to assess the national territory and invite transnational companies to explore and drill into our soil in search of the oil we need to survive? Is this the socialism we wanted? But since we know that to build socialism, the homeland is needed, the Revolution is needed to preserve the homeland, and the Revolution is needed to preserve the best conquests and the hopes of socialism.

We will preserve those hopes, and the socialism we build will be perfected.

Can a Revolutionary Process be Reversed?

Speech delivered at the commemoration of the 60th anniversary of Fidel's admission to the University of Havana, held in the Aula Magna of the University of Havana, on 17 November 2005, during the Year of the Bolivarian Alternative for the Americas.

DEAR STUDENTS AND professors from universities from all over Cuba;

Dear comrades, leaders, and guests who have shared with us so many years of struggle:

This is the most difficult moment when I must say some words in this great hall, where many words have already been spoken. A universe of ideas comes to mind, and it's only logical because time has passed.

You have been very kind to remember that today is a very special day: the 60th anniversary of my timid entry into this university.

There is a photo somewhere, and I was looking at it: I was wearing a jacket, and I have an angry, or a tough, or a nice, or an irritated face because that photo was not taken on the first day; I think I had already been here for several months, and I was starting to react to so many things that were happening then. It was not a deep-seated thought. There was this eagerness for ideas, a desire to learn, and a spirit that was perhaps rebellious. We were full of dreams that couldn't be described as revolutionary but were undoubtedly full of illusions and energy, and possibly also anxiety to take up a struggle.

I had been active in sports, and I had climbed mountains. I had even been promoted to some Boy Scout lieutenant; I'm not exactly sure why, and later on, they made me a general of the Boy Scouts. So, when I was in high school, I had been given more ranks than I have today. Because later, I became Comandante, but nothing more than Comandante; this thing of being *Comandante en jefe* doesn't mean anything more than being the chief commander of that small troop of about eighty-two men, the men who came in the *Granma* yacht.

That title came up after the landing on 2 December 1956. There had to be a chief among those eighty-two men. Later, they added the 'in'; little by little, I went from being Chief Commander to being the Commander-in-Chief as we had more commanders because, for a long time, that was the highest rank. I was remembering these things; one must think about what one was, what one thought about, and what feelings one had.

Perhaps some specific circumstances in my life made me react; I had to face difficulties from a very early age, and maybe because of that, I grew up to be a professional rebel.

I've heard talk about rebels without a cause; but I seem to remember, whenever I think about it, that I was a rebel with many causes. I thank life that I have continued being a rebel over the years, even today, perhaps more rightly so today, because I have many more ideas and more experience. I have learned a lot from my struggle, and I have a better understanding of this country where we were all born and of this world where we live, this globalized world living now in a decisive time for its destiny. I wouldn't dare say a decisive time in its history because its history is shorter, really brief when compared to the life span of a species that in recent times—perhaps 3,000 or 4,000 or 5,000 years ago—took its first steps after its long and brief evolution. I say long and brief because life evolved to the point of becoming homo sapiens some hundreds of thousands of years after life came into existence on this planet, as scholars believe it to be. If my memory doesn't fail me, around 1 or 1.5 billion years ago, a life form was born and after that came millions of species. And we are only that; we are one of the species born on this planet. And that is why I said, after a brief and at the same time long life, we have come to this point, in this millennium, which is said to be the third millennium since the beginning of the Christian era.

Why am I circling around this idea? Because I would dare say that today this species is facing a real danger of extinction, and no one can be sure, listen to this well, no one can be sure that it will survive this danger.

Well, the fact that the species would not survive was discussed 2,000 years ago. When I was a student, I heard of the Apocalypse, a book of prophecy in the Bible; 2,000 years ago, someone realized that this vulnerable species could one day disappear.

Of course, so did the Marxists. I remember Engel's book *Dialectics of Nature* very well; he said that one day the light of the sun would go out, that the fuel feeding the fires of that star, which illuminates our world, would run out, and the light of the sun would cease to exist. So, a question remains in my mind; a question that maybe you, your professors, hundreds of thousands of you have also asked yourselves, and that is: if there is any possibility that this species can emigrate to another solar system?

Have you never asked yourselves that question? Well, at some point, you will, because many questions come to our minds during our lifetime, particularly these questions, which usually are asked when there is a reason to do so. I believe that humanity never had more reasons than it does now to wonder about this; because if that Marxist considered the problem of solar heat and light disappearing, and if that scientist considered that one day the solar system would cease to exist, we too, as revolutionaries, giving wings to our imaginations, must ask ourselves what will happen and if there is any hope for this species to escape to another solar system where life already exists or could exist. All that we know today is that there is one sun four light-years away, among the billions of suns that exist in that enormous outer space of which we still don't know whether it is finite or infinite.

We have been speaking of events in our lives, in our university, in our alma mater, about those of us who came here a few decades ago and who are present here today, those who are in their first year or are about to graduate, or those who have already graduated and are engaged in tasks that others with less experience would not be able to do.

I have many events to attend every day, and I am speaking with large groups for hours and hours on end, especially with groups of young people, students, with medical brigades who go out to work in glorious missions that almost nobody else in this world would discharge, because no other country could send 1,000 medical doctors to a sister nation in Central America. We have sent just such a group that is now confronting pain and death in the aftermath of the greatest natural tragedy that anyone in that country can remember.

One after another, I have been speaking to these brigades, and I've been seeing them off; the same with those who are leaving for the other side of the world, flying for eighteen hours, to where almost simultaneously another of the greatest human tragedies struck. I remember no other catastrophe of such dimensions because of the place it hit and the affected humble people; these people are shepherds living on very high mountains. The tragedy struck on the eve of winter, where the cold is most intense and poverty immense. While the insensitive world that wastes a trillion dollars each year on advertising to bamboozle the majority of humanity who are deceived into paying to spread these lies, depriving these human beings of the capacity to think for themselves, forced to buy a soap that is the same soap with ten different names, and who must be deceived because a trillion dollars are spent on it. The companies do not pay this money; it is paid by those who buy the product due to the advertising.

This insensitive world that spends one trillion dollars each year on the military—it's already two trillion—this insensitive world that extracts trillions of dollars a year from the impoverished masses, from the immense majority of this planet's inhabitants, remains indifferent when it's told that around 100,000 people have died, among them maybe 25,000 or 30,000 children, or that there are 100,000 injured. The large majority is suffering from bone fractures in their arms and legs, of which barely 10 per cent have been operated on, that there are children with mutilated limbs, as well as young people, women and men, and older people.

This is the kind of world we live in; it is not a world full of goodness but a world full of egoism. It is not a world of justice but one full of exploitation, abuse, and pillage. Millions of children die every year—where they could be saved—just because they lack a few cents worth of medicine, or some vitamins, or rehydration salts—and a few dollars' worth of food, enough for them to live. They die every year due to injustice; almost as many died in that colossal war that I mentioned a few minutes ago.

What kind of world is this? What kind of world is this where a barbaric empire proclaims its right to launch pre-emptive attacks on seventy or more countries and can bring death to any corner of the globe, using the most sophisticated weapons and killing techniques? It's a world where brutality and force prevail, with hundreds of military bases on the entire planet. There is one of these on our soil, where they arbitrarily intervened after the Spanish colonial power could no longer stand by itself, and when hundreds of thousands of our country's dearest sons and daughters in a population of hardly a million, had perished in a long war lasting almost thirty years. And they left us with the revolting Platt Amendment, attached to an equally repugnant resolution that treacherously gave them the right to intervene in our country whenever they considered there to be a lack of order.

More than a century has gone by, and this piece of our territory is still forcibly occupied today, known to have been turned into a torture centre, where hundreds of people pulled in from different parts of the world are kept in detention, bringing shame and horror to the world. They do not take them to their own country because there may be laws that would make things difficult for them to illegally hold these people by force, kidnapped for years, overriding any legal procedure, and to the amazement of the entire world, these people are being subjected to sadistic and brutal torture. The world learned of this only when, in Iraq, they were torturing hundreds of prisoners from a country invaded by the powerful forces of a colossal empire and where hundreds of thousands of Iraqi civilians have lost their lives.

New things come up every day; recently, the press reported that the US government had secret prisons in the satellite countries of Eastern Europe, the same countries that vote in Geneva against Cuba and accuse us of human rights violations. They accuse the country that has never known a torture centre in forty-six years of Revolution because our country has never broken that unparalleled tradition in history where even one person has been known to be tortured. And we would not be the only ones preventing that; it would be our people who acquired the loftiest concept of human dignity a long time ago.

As the son of a landowner, I was able to complete sixth grade, and when I graduated from seventh grade, I could enrol in a senior high school. If you couldn't attend high school, you couldn't go on to university. The children of farmers or workers, living at the sugar mills or in a municipality, unless it was a municipality in Santiago or Holguin or Manzanillo, or a few others, couldn't go to high school, not even high school! Of course, that left them without the possibility of graduating from university because, after high school, you had to come to Havana for further studies.

I could come to Havana because my father had the means to send me, so I graduated from high school, and fortune led me to university. Did that mean that I was better than any of the hundreds of boys, few of whom completed the sixth grade and none of whom graduated from high school or went to university?

Before the Revolution, many noble students were opposing the Batista tyranny and willing to make sacrifices, willing to die. And so, when the Batista tyranny returned with a vengeance, many students fought, and many students died. That young man from Cárdenas, Manzanita as he was called, always smiling, jovial, and affectionate with everyone, became well-known for his bravery and integrity when he descended the university stairs, facing the water hose of the fire trucks or the police. That is how all of them came to be known.

If you visit the house where Jose Antonio Echevarria lived—Jose Antonio, we'll call him—you'll see that it is a good house, an excellent house. You could see how the students were often oblivious to their social or class origins at that age of so many hopes and dreams.

There was only one medical faculty and one teaching hospital at that university, yet many students received prizes and awards, first prize in medicine and even in surgery without ever having operated on anybody.

Some others made an effort; they were active and contacted a professor who helped them, taking part in their practice or at some hospital. That's how there were good doctors, not a huge number of good doctors; indeed, there was a massive number of doctors who wanted to travel to the United States; they were unemployed, and with the triumph of the Revolution, that's where they went, straight to the USA, and Cuba was left with half of all our medical doctors—3,000 of them—and 25 per cent of our professors. That's the point at which we started, and yet today, we stand up, almost like the capital of world medicine.

Today, our people have at their disposal at least fifteen doctors for everyone that remained in the country, and they are much better distributed. Cuba has thousands of doctors abroad fraternally offering their services, and the number is growing. At this time, and I specifically asked for the exact figure, we have 25,000 medical students; in the first year, there are about 7,000, and each year there will be at least 7,000 more; we have more than 70,000 medical student doctors. There are also tens of thousands of students in other medical sciences. We believe that there are 90,000 studying in the medical field if we include students majoring in nursing and other health sector professions. All of them are part of a large number of students in our universities today.

I wanted to bring up the differences from when I entered university; what was our country like then? We should ask ourselves that question and meditate on it. What is our country like today, in all areas? And we could ask the same question about eight, ten, fifteen, twenty different things; comparison is impossible!

We came to the university at the end of 1945, and only eight years later, we began the armed struggle in the Moncada Barracks on 26 July 1953. The Revolution triumphed five years, five months, and five days after Moncada, after a long journey through prison, exile, and fighting in the mountains. It was a relatively short time, historically speaking, comparing it to earlier struggles that were so difficult on our people. There were two stages—coming to the university and leaving it—and the *coup d'état* on 10 March 1952.

The stage when we began the struggle is where we will start now. We set off, and we attempted to set off, not being too knowledgeable about the laws of gravity. We headed upwards, struggling against the empire that was already the most powerful one, but then another superpower also existed; we continued marching upwards, gaining experience, seeing our people and the Revolution gain in strength, until this point where we are today.

I wish I had more time to speak to you, but this moment now is without precedent—it is a time that is different from all the others. It is nothing like it was in 1945; it is nothing like it was in 1950 when we graduated; but we had all those ideas that I mentioned before when I affirmed with love, respect, and the utmost affection that I came to this university with a rebellious spirit, with some elemental ideas of justice. Here I became a revolutionary; I became a Marxist-Leninist; and I acquired the ideas that I have never abandoned, nor have I ever been tempted to do so, not in the least. For that reason, I dare say that I will never abandon them.

In the spirit of confession, I could say that when I finished studying at this university, I thought I was very revolutionary, although basically, I was just starting on a much longer path. At that time, I felt that I was a revolutionary or a socialist. I had absorbed all the ideas that made me who I am, and I could be nothing other than a revolutionary. Today, in all modesty, I assure you that I feel ten times, twenty times, even a hundred times more revolutionary today than I was then. If I was willing to give up my life at that time, today, I am a thousand times more willing to give up my life for the Revolution.

You are constantly reading the works of the great thinkers; you are continually reading history. Regarding our country's history, you read the works of Martì, and you read the works of many distinguished patriots; and regarding the history of the world and the history of the revolutionary movements, you read the theoreticians, those great theoreticians, who never faltered in their revolutionary principles. The ideas bring us together; ideas make us combatant people on a collective and not just an individual basis—ideas make us a mass of revolutionaries. Then, when all the forces unite, the people can never be defeated; and when the number of ideas grows, when the number of ideas and values to be defended grows and multiplies, that is when a people can truly never be defeated.

And so, when we remember our comrades, and we see the youth who are taking on such important tasks, we must also remember that many of the others were leaders in this university who had struggled for many years, some for more than fifty, others might have struggled for more than forty, and today each one has his responsibility. Many of them are students, and others come from humble backgrounds. I see them all here today, those who were at Moncada, those that came on the *Granma*, those who fought in the Sierra Maestra and participated in all the battles. I see them all here, each one of them, defending a cause, a flag.

I see, for example, our dear comrade Alarcon. I remember him because here we have been speaking of the struggle for the five imprisoned heroes, and he has been their indefatigable champion for justice. This was the task given him by the Revolution, and he has shouldered the responsibility with his talent and in his capacity as President of the National Assembly.

I see comrade Machadito, a former doctor, but not an old doctor, who was with us in the mountains. I see Lazo, Lage, and Balaguer; I see many more out there, I still have good sight. I think I see Saez, and I think we can see the Minister of Higher Education. I think I can see Gomez, with a few more pounds perhaps; further along, I see Abel with a biblical name, who has just come back from Mar del Plata where he waged a glorious battle.

Look at this world and see all the changes, all the aims we are pursuing today. Look at the strategies that are being designed against us. We are a tiny country, ninety miles away from the colossal empire, the most powerful empire ever in the history of the world. Forty-five years have passed, and there it is, farther away than ever from the possibility of forcing the Cuban nation to its knees, the same nation they humiliated and offended for some time. Once, the US owned everything in Cuba: the mines, hundreds of thousands of the best hectares of land, the ports and its facilities, the electrical system, transportation, banking, commercial activities, etc. And these idiots believe that they will return here and that we will call to them on bended knees: 'Come and save us again, Oh Saviours of the World! Come, and we shall again give you everything we have, this university too so that you can put in five thousand instead of half a million students; half a million is too much, and with your mentality, you would like to see us unemployed and hungry so that filthy capitalism can function because it is only with a reserve corps of unemployed that it can function; come back and make the ranks of our illiterate and unemployed grow and stand in lines by the sugarcane fields with nobody bringing them water to drink, or food to eat, or housing, or transportation. Look for them, see if you can find them because here are their children, hundreds of thousands of them studying in the universities'.

I think it was Agramonte, and others say it was Cespedes, who responded to the pessimists when he had just twelve men with him: 'I don't care about those lacking in confidence, because with these twelve men I can make a nation'. If a nation can be made with twelve men, how many times greater than twelve men are we today? And twelve men, many times multiplied, armed with ideas, knowledge, culture, knowing all about the world, knowing about history, geography, about the struggles, because they possess what we call a revolutionary conscience, which is the sum total of many consciences; it is the sum total of a humanist conscience, the conscience of honour and dignity and the best values that man can grow. This nation is born of love for the homeland and love for the world; we cannot forget that the homeland is humanity, a statement made more than a hundred years ago. Homeland is humanity, and we must repeat that every day, when someone forgets those living in Haiti or Guatemala, suffering from the ravages of a natural disaster, among other things, suffering indescribable pain and indescribable poverty, as it is usually the case in most parts of the world.

That is all that the infamous empire, and its repugnant system, can show as a result of a history where the species set out on a long march for a just society that has not been attained over thousands of years, which is the very short, relatively well-known history of a species in its quest for a just society. And they have always been as far away from that society as we are close to it today, that is, closer to that just society we want to construct. And I dare say that regardless of the many flaws we still have, of our errors and inefficiencies, this is the society that comes closer to being described as a just society in all human history.

Where is justice that I cannot see it? I cannot see it because that one over there earns twenty, thirty times more than me as a doctor, or more than me as an engineer, or more than me as a university professor. Where is justice? And why is this happening? What does the other produce? How many does he educate? How many does he heal? How many are made happy with his knowledge, his books, and his art? How many does he make happy by building a home? How many does he make happy by growing something to eat? How many does he make happy by working in factories, in industries, in the electrical system, in the drinking water system, in the streets, on the power grids, looking after communications or printing books? How many?

We must say that there are several dozens of thousands of parasites who produce nothing. Just take that individual driving a vintage car from Havana to Guantanamo, buying and stealing fuel all along the way, who charged one of those young students 1,000 pesos, 1,200 pesos, when he was forced to travel at a time when transportation difficulties were at their greatest. He knows his way alongside those highways, full of potholes in many places and missing a lot of signals; things that couldn't be finished for a variety of reasons, because of resources we lack, for conditions we still haven't been able to fix, and for lack of controls over the managers and other staffs.

Yes, we must bear that in mind and not forget it, for we are faced with a great battle, which we must begin to undertake. We shall undertake it, and we will win it. That's what is most important.

Yes, we are very much aware of this, and we think about this more than about anything else: our flaws, our mistakes, our inequalities, our injustice.

I wouldn't dare to mention this subject here if I was not firmly convinced and sure that we are quickly getting closer to reducing them and to obliterating them so that, barring world catastrophes and colossal wars, we can truly accomplish something. Listen to this well: our country's citizens, who at one time, suffered a 10 per cent, 15 per cent, 20 per cent or more rate of unemployment; our citizens who, at one time, numbered one million illiterate people, some being illiterate and some being semi-literate, up to 90 per cent of the population; this nation today, and in the very near future, will have every one of her citizens living fundamentally off their work and their pensions and retirement incomes.

Never forget our working class, those who for decades went through sacrifice—suffering the attacks of mercenary bands in the mountains, invasions like Giron, thousands of acts of sabotage that killed our sugar cane workers, our industrial and factory workers, those in the merchant marine or the fishing industry, those who were suddenly attacked with cannons and bazookas—only because they were Cuban, only because they wanted to be independent, only because they wanted to improve the fate of our people. There were the bandits, doing as they pleased, those bandits recruited and trained by the CIA. Some are criminals, some are terrorists who blew up planes in mid-air or attempted to blow them up, indifferent to how many would die, and those over there who organize attacks of every kind and organize acts of terrorism against our country.

Some speak of the battle of ideas, that battle of ideas, which we have been waging for several years now, and which is becoming a battle of ideas throughout the world. These ideas will triumph; these ideas must triumph. Let's carry this message; let's open the eyes of a humanity that seems condemned to extinction. It won't be eternal, as it is very likely that even the light of the sun will go out one day. It is almost certain that there will be no way to move the living, solid matter to a distance that is light years away from Earth; the laws of physics are much more rigorous, much more exact than historical or social laws.

In any case, I believe that this humanity and all the great things it is capable of creating must be preserved while it is still possible to do so. A humanity that doesn't care about the preservation of its species would be like the young student or leader, who knows that his life is very limited to just a few short years and, nevertheless, worries only about his existence.

In this battle against vice, there will be no truce for anyone, and we shall be thoroughly scrupulous. We will appeal to everyone's sense of honour. We are sure of one thing: every human being possesses a healthy dose of honour. When one looks in the mirror, one is not always the harshest of judges, even though, in my opinion, the first responsibility of a revolutionary is to be extremely severe with oneself.

We are speaking of criticism and self-criticism, that's true, but our criticisms tend to be almost always in groups; we never resort to criticism in a wider circle; we never resort to criticism on a larger scale.

For example, if a Public Health official fudges the data documenting the existence of the Aedes Aegypti mosquito, he is summoned, he is criticized. I know some people who say: 'Yes, of course, I criticize myself.' And with that, they are content. What a laugh! They are actually happy. So, you criticize yourself, and what about all the harm you have caused and the millions that were lost because you were careless or acted incorrectly?

Criticism and self-criticism, it's all very good, as it did not exist in the past. However, if we are going to war, we need weapons of greater calibre; we must carry out criticism and self-criticism in the schoolroom, in the party cells, and then outside the party cells, in the municipality, and finally in the entire country.

Let's make use of that sense of honour which, undoubtedly, we all have, because I know many who are what we call 'shameless' people, and they truly are shameless, but when in some local newspaper they report what this individual has done, they are filled with shame.

The Revolution has to use these weapons, and we shall use them whenever necessary! It shouldn't have to be necessary. The Revolution will establish the necessary controls.

After many years, here is a conclusion I've come to: among all the errors we may have committed, the greatest of them all was that we believed that someone really knew something about socialism or that someone actually knew how to build socialism. It seemed to be a sure fact, as well-known as the electrical system conceived by those who thought they were experts in electrical systems. Whenever they said: 'That's the formula', we thought they knew. Just as if someone is a physician. You are not going to debate anaemia, intestinal problems, or any other condition with a physician; nobody argues with the physician. You can think that he is a good doctor or a bad one, you can follow his advice or not, but you won't argue with him. Which of us would argue with a doctor, a mathematician, a historian, an expert in literature, or any other subject? But we must be idiots if we think, for example, that economics is an exact and eternal science and that it has existed since the days of Adam and Eve, and I offer my apologies to the thousands of economists in our country.

All sense of dialectics is lost when someone believes that today's economy is identical to the economy of 50, 100 or 150 years ago, or that it is identical to the one during Lenin's time or to the time when Karl Marx lived. Revisionism is a thousand miles away from my mind, and I genuinely revere Marx, Engels, and Lenin.

One day I said: 'I became a revolutionary in this university'; it was because I encountered those books. Well before I had committed myself, without having read any of those books, I was questioning capitalist political economy. Even at that time, it all seemed irrational to me. So, I took a political economy course in the first year, taught by Portela, with 900 mimeographed pages to read; it was really difficult; almost everyone failed. What a holy terror that professor was!

It was that class that explained the laws of capitalism and

examined the various theories about the origin of value; it also mentioned the Marxists, the Utopians, the Communists, in short, every economic theory. But once I began to study the political economy of capitalism, I began to have great doubts, and I began to question all that because I had grown up on a large rural estate and I remembered things; I had spontaneous ideas, just as any other utopian in this world.

Then, once I learned what utopian communism was, I realized that I was a utopian communist because all my ideas took off from the idea: 'This is not good, this is bad, this is a crime. How can we possibly have an overproduction and hunger crisis simultaneously, when there is more coal, colder winters, more unemployed, because there is more capacity to create wealth? Wouldn't it be simpler to produce and distribute the wealth?'

Just as Karl Marx thought in the period when he wrote the *Critique of the Gotha Program*, it seemed like limits for abundance were inherent in the capitalist social system; it seemed that just as the productive forces developed, they could produce everything that the human being needed to satisfy all his essential requirements almost limitlessly, be they material, cultural, etc.

We have all read that *Program*, and it is certainly very respectable. It established with total clarity the difference in concept between socialist distribution and communist distribution. Marx didn't like to play the prophet or paint pictures of the future; he was very serious and would never have done that.

When he wrote political books like the *18th Brumaire* and the *Civil War in France*, he was a genius with a crystal-clear interpretation. His *Communist Manifesto* is a classic. You can analyze it and be more or less satisfied with this and with that. I moved on from utopian communism to a communism that was based on serious social development theories, such as dialectic materialism. There was a lot of philosophy, much fighting and arguing. But of course, it is important to pay close attention to different philosophical tendencies.

In our real world, which must be changed, every revolutionary tactician and strategist has an obligation to conceive of a strategy and a tactic that will lead to the fundamental objective, to change the real world. No divisive tactic or strategy can be a good one.

The world is desperately crying out for unity, and if we cannot achieve a minimum of unity, we will not go anywhere.

I don't know why the communists were credited with the philosophy that the ends justify the means, and sometimes one even asks oneself why the communists didn't defend themselves from that accusation of the ends justifying the means. My explanation is that it is due to historical reasons. There was an enormous influence exerted by the first socialist state and by the first true socialist revolution born in a feudal country that still, by and large, has feudal customs and habits and a large percentage of illiteracy. Still, it was the first working-class revolution springing from the ideas of Marx and Engels and developed by the other great genius, Lenin.

Above all, Lenin studied State issues; Marx did not speak of the worker–peasant alliance because he lived in a country that had a highly developed industrial base. Lenin recognized the under-developed world; he understood that the country was composed of 80 to 90 per cent peasants, and even though there was a strong proletariat presence in the railroad and other industries, Lenin saw with utmost clarity the necessity to forge a worker–peasant alliance. No one before had spoken of this; they had philosophized, but they hadn't talked about it. The first socialist revolution, the first real attempt at a just and egalitarian society, takes place in a vast, semi-feudal, semi-underdeveloped country. None of the previous societies, slave-based, feudal, medieval, anti-feudal, bourgeois, or capitalist, could ever propose the existence of a just society even though much was said about liberty, equality, and fraternity.

Throughout history, the first serious human attempt to create the first just society began less than two hundred years ago; the *Communist Manifesto* was written in 1848 and in forty-five years, yes, in forty-five more years, it will be 200 years old. After it was written, the evolution of revolutionary thinking could be appreciated.

One could never have arrived at a strategy through dogma. Lenin taught us a lot because Marx taught us to understand society. Lenin taught us to understand the state and the role of the state.

All these historical factors had a tremendous influence on revolutionary thinking, and of course, there were abusive practices, sometimes even repugnant ones.

This gave rise to the slanderous accusation that for communists, 'the ends justify the means'. I have reflected a great deal about the role of ethics. What is the ethic of a revolutionary? All revolutionary thinking begins with ethics; some values are acquired from parents, others from teachers, but no one is born with these ideas. No one is born with the gift of speech either, and someone has to teach us to speak. The influence of the family is huge.

We were speaking of the importance of the ethical factor. We would have to research the reasons for the confusion. I believe that historical events influenced the idea that for a communist, the ends justify the means. There were international events that were difficult to understand. I've mentioned them on more than one occasion; despite everything, there was the precedent of France and Britain, those two great colonial powers and the greatest in the world, attempting to hurl Hitler against the USSR. I think the imperialist plans to throw Hitler against the USSR would never have justified the pact between Hitler and Stalin; it was a tough blow. The communist parties, well-known for their discipline, were obliged to defend the Molotov–Ribbentrop Pact and bleed to death politically.

Before this pact, the necessity for unification in the anti-fascist struggle led to the alliance in Cuba of the Cuban communists with Batista. By then, Batista had suppressed the famous strike of April 1934 that followed his coup against the provisional government in 1933, which was unquestionably revolutionary and largely the result of the historical fight of the workers' movement and the Cuban communists. Before that anti-fascist alliance, Batista had assassinated countless people, robbed Cuba of incredible sums of money, and became the flunky of Yankee imperialism. The order came from Moscow: organize the anti-fascist front. It was a pact with the devil. Here the pact was with the fascist ABC and Batista, a fascist of a different colour, who was both a criminal and robber of the public coffer.

These were challenging events, and one followed on the heels of another; the most disciplined communists in the world, and I say that with all sincere respect, were the communist parties of Latin America, among these, was the Cuban Communist Party, and I have always held them in very high regard, and I still do.

Today we can speak of this subject because we are entering a new phase.

The members of the Cuban Communist Party were the most disciplined people, the most honourable and the most self-sacrificing for this country. The Party legislators handed over a portion of their salaries. They were the most honourable people in the country, notwithstanding the erroneous direction Stalin imposed on the international movement. How can we blame them? They were faced with the dilemma of accepting or not something which was, in my criteria, absolutely correct: the unity of all communists. 'Workers of the world, unite!', or openly destroy, under the circumstances, all discipline.

I am not one of those people who criticize historical characters demonized by world reaction so that they become a joke for the bourgeoisie and the imperialists. Nor am I going to commit the stupidity of not daring to say what needs to be said on a day like today. We must have the courage to recognize our own errors precisely for that reason, for only in that manner will we reach the objective that we hope to attain. A tremendous vice was created, the abuse of power, the cruelty and, in particular, the habit of one country imposing its authority, that of one hegemonic party, over all other countries and parties.

For more than forty years, we have maintained relations with the Latin American revolutionary movement, and they have been extremely close relations. However, it has never even occurred to us to tell anybody what they should be doing; we have seen every revolutionary movement zealously defend its rights and prerogatives.

I remember crucial moments, I will state this here, and it will only be part of the story. When the USSR crumbled, many people were left on their own, including the Cuban revolutionaries, but we knew what we had to do, what our options were. Everywhere, revolutionary movements were carrying on their struggle; I am not going to say which ones, I'm not going to say who they were, but they were all very serious revolutionary movements. They asked us whether there should be some negotiation process in the face of such a desperate situation, whether the struggle should continue or not, whether negotiations should begin with the other side to strike a peace accord, even though everyone knew the consequences of such a peace.

I would tell them: 'You cannot ask us our opinion, as it will be you fighting the battle, and you alone who will die, not us. We know what we are going to do and what we are prepared to do, but these are decisions which each one must make for themselves'. That was the highest expression of our respect for the other movements. We have never attempted to impose ourselves on the basis of our knowledge and experience or due to the enormous respect they show for our Revolution, which motivated them to listen to our point of view.

At that moment, we didn't know whether there would be advantages or disadvantages for Cuba as a result of the decisions that they would take: 'You make your own decisions', we said. And so, at the decisive moment, each one of them charted their own path. We are a small island here in the Caribbean, ninety miles away from the empire and within inches of their illegal military base, a thousand times weaker than the USSR at the time of its pact with Hitler, or at the time it was giving orders to the communist parties. The Nazis invaded Poland, and the Soviet army had been purged of its best and most brilliant leaders due to scheming by the Nazis. At the time of the Weimar Republic established in Germany after World War I, amid a tremendous economic crisis unleashed as a consequence of the Treaty of Versailles imposed by England, France, and the United States, there was in Germany a strengthening of the revolutionary movement and growth of the most reactionary nationalist forces.

Hitler wins in the elections against the liberal bourgeois parties and the militant communist and revolutionary forces. But a much more decisive factor was the terrible resentment of the German people against those unfair conditions dictated by the victors. And it is against this background that Hitler comes to power. In a book he wrote, Hitler casually declared that he aimed to seek vital living space in USSR territory for the German race, at the expense of the Russians, whom he considered being an inferior race. All this was written, and the communist movement took on very clear ideas and concepts to oppose Nazi fascism.

After so many revolutionaries had fallen in our country, since the communists were the most conscientious, the most militant and the most honourable, the Marxist-Leninist Party was led, of course, to that alliance with Batista, the same who had repressed students and the public in general. The young people resented his power very much; the workers who had always seen their interests continuously defended by the communist leaders were firmly loyal to the party, but it was among the youth and popular sections of society that there was the most justified rejection of Batista.

I believe that the experience of that first socialist state, a state that should have been fixed and not destroyed, was a bitter one. You may be sure that we have thought many times about that incredible phenomenon where one of the mightiest powers in the world disintegrated the way it did; for this was a power that had matched the strength of the other superpower and had paid with the lives of more than twenty million of her people in the battle against fascism.

Is it that revolutions are doomed to fall apart, or that people cause revolutions to fall apart? Can either humans or society prevent revolutions from collapsing? I could immediately add to this another question: Do you believe that this revolutionary socialist process can fall apart or not? Have you ever given that some thought? Have you ever deeply reflected on it?

Were you aware of all these inequalities that I have been talking about? Were you aware of certain generalized habits? Did you know that there are people who earn forty or fifty times the amount one of those doctors over there in the mountains of Guatemala, part of the Henry Reeve Medical Contingent, earns in one month? Our doctors could be in other faraway reaches of Africa, or at an altitude of thousands of metres, in the Himalayas, saving lives and earning 5 per cent or 10 per cent of what one of those dirty little crooks earns, selling gasoline to the new rich, diverting resources from the ports in trucks and by the ton load, stealing in the dollar shops, stealing in a five-star hotel by exchanging a bottle of rum for another of lesser quality and pocketing the dollars for which he sells the drinks.

Just how many ways of stealing do we have in this country? Why do we read every day in the opinion polls that people ask when are the 'kids' coming to the dollar stores, drugstores, or other places? Everyone is full of admiration for these 'kids', the social workers. They've come from economically disadvantaged environments and are now highly prepared and trained.

I looked at those faces as I look at you now, and faces tell me more than any article, book, or cliché can. You are aware that there has been a class difference since the beginning of civilization, since the inception of private property. The world has only known a class-based society; all the rest is pre-history.

How is it that I can tell that you come from economically disadvantaged environments? None of you entered university because you were the son or daughter of a prosperous landowner.

Here we are, and I have been given the honour of sitting here. Which of you has a father who owns 1,000 hectares or more than 10,000 hectares? I won't ask each of you because all I need to do is to look at you to know whether, by chance, one of you is the child of some professional of the middle class. You applauded loudly because I know where you are coming from, and you know that today, there is no one left that cuts sugar cane by hand. Who were the cane cutters?

I could also explain why we no longer cut cane today; there are no cane cutters here, and the heavy machinery destroys the sugar cane fields. The abuses of the developed world and the subsidies have led to sugar prices crashing to the bottom of the trash barrel on the world markets. In the meantime, Europe was paying its growers two or three times more.

In the days when the USSR paid 27 or 28 cents for our sugar but paid in oil because it was cheaper to pay for sugar with oil than to buy the beet sugar produced labour intensively in the Russian fields, the USSR was a country whose economy grew extensively, not intensively, and so their labour force was never enough, and the beet harvest required many workers.

So, we are now coming to the point of asking ourselves this question—I have already reached this point myself, some years ago—in the face of this super powerful empire that stalks us and threatens us, and that has transition plans and military action plans in this specific historical moment.

They are awaiting a natural and logical event, the death of someone; in this case, they have honoured me by thinking of me. It might be a confession of what they have not been able to do in a long time. If I were a vain man, I could be proud of the fact that those guys admit that they are waiting for me to die, and this is the time. They are waiting for me to die, and every day they invent something new: 'Castro has this, he's suffering from that', and now the latest is that they say, 'Castro has Parkinson's disease'.

I once said that the day I die, nobody will believe it; I'll probably carry on like El Cid, astride his horse, winning battles, even after death.

You can never trust imperialism; it is treacherous and capable of anything. It tortures in Guantanamo; it tortures in the prisons of Iraq; it has prisons for torture in the former socialist countries; it uses live phosphorus, and then it says: 'It is the most innocent and legitimate of weapons'. If you were in my position, it would be logical for you to have a weapon and be able to use it. And so, I do. I have a Browning with a 15-shot capacity. I've used guns a lot in my life.

I asked you a question, comrade students; don't worry, I haven't forgotten, and I'd like to believe that you will never forget it. It is the question that I ask in view of the historical experiences we have known, and I ask you all, without exception, to reflect on it: Can the revolutionary process be irreversible, or not? Which are the ideas or the degree of conscience that would make the reversal of the revolutionary process impossible? When those who were the forerunners, the veterans, start disappearing and making room for new generations of leaders, what will be done, and how will it be accomplished? After all, we have been witnesses to many errors, and we didn't notice.

A leader has tremendous power when he enjoys the confidence of the masses that put complete trust in his abilities. The consequences of errors committed by those in authority are terrible, and this has happened more than once during the revolutionary processes.

Such is the stuff for meditation. One studies history; and one meditates on what happened here and there, on what happened today and on what will happen tomorrow, on where each country's processes will lead, what path our own process will take, how it will get there, and what role Cuba will play in this process.

The country has endured limitations in resources, many limitations, but this country has also wasted resources thoughtlessly. So, while you received the soaps that had no perfume and the toothpaste, regularly every month, and even though sometimes certain activities in the schools were neglected which, for example, caused the excellent state of dental health among our youth to decay, some thought that socialism could be constructed with capitalist methods. That is one of the great historical errors; I do not wish to speak of this, and I don't want to theorize. But I have an infinite number of examples of many things that couldn't be resolved by those who called themselves theoreticians, blanketing themselves from head to toe in the books of Marx, Engels, Lenin, and many others.

That's why I commented that: One of our greatest mistakes at the beginning of, and often during, the Revolution was believing that someone knew how to build socialism.

In my opinion, today, we have relatively clear ideas about how one goes about building socialism, but we need many extremely clear ideas and many questions answered by you who will be the ones responsible for the preservation, or not, of socialism in the future.

What kind of a society would this be; how worthy of joy could we be when we assemble on a day like today, in a place like this, if we were not minimally aware of what we need to know, so that on our heroic island, these heroic people, this nation, which has written pages in the history books like no other nation in the history of humanity, can preserve the Revolution? Please, do not think that who is speaking to you is a vain man or a charlatan, or someone inclined to bluff.

Forty-six years have passed, and the history of this country is known, and the people of this nation know it well. They also know their neighbour very well—the empire—with its size and its power, its strength and its wealth, its technology, and its control over the World Bank, the International Monetary Fund, and all the world of finances. That country has imposed on us the most incredibly iron-clad blockade, which was discussed at the United Nations, where 182 nations supported Cuba, voting freely even though they ran a risk of voting against the empire. The island has achieved this today, not during the days when the European socialist countries stood together with us, but after the socialist camp had disappeared and the USSR had fallen apart. We forged this Revolution alone, against all risk, for many long years; and we realized that if the day ever came when we would be under direct attack by the US, no one would ever fight for us, nor would we ask anyone to do so.

It would have been naïve of us to think, or to ask for, or to expect that one superpower would fight against the other, in this day and age of modern technological development, to intervene on this island ninety miles away. We concluded that such support would never happen. And another thing, once we asked them directly, a few years before the collapse: 'Tell us frankly'. 'No', they said. It was the answer we knew they would give, and from that point on, more than ever, we accelerated the development of our concept, and we perfected the tactical and strategic ideas that have led to the triumph and victory of the Revolution. The Revolution's strength began with the struggle of seven armed men against an enemy with 80,000 troops, including marines, soldiers and police, tanks, airplanes, and all kinds of modern weaponry of that time. What an infinitely huge difference between our weapons and the weapons of that army, trained by the US, supported by the US, and supplied by the US. After we received our reply, we held on to our concepts more firmly than ever; we deepened them; and we gained in strength to the point where we can affirm today that our country is militarily invulnerable, not because of arms of mass destruction.

They may have tanks to spare, but we have just what we need, not one to spare! All their technology collapses like ice-cubes beneath the noon-day sun in a hot summer. And again, just like when we possessed only seven guns and a handful of bullets, today, we possess much more than those seven guns. We have a people who have learned to handle weapons; we have an entire nation that, despite our errors, holds such a high degree of culture, education, and conscience that it will never allow this country to become a US colony again.

This country can self-destruct; this Revolution can destroy itself, but they can never destroy us; only we can destroy ourselves, and it would be our fault.

I have been fortunate to have lived many years. That is not a special merit but rather, it is an exceptional opportunity to share with you everything that I am telling you—young leaders, all the leaders of the masses, all the leaders of the workers' movement, the Committees for the Defense of the Revolution, the women's groups, the farmers, and the veterans of the Revolution—who have organized throughout the country hundreds of thousands who have struggled through the years carrying out glorious internationalist missions, students like yourselves, intelligent, well prepared, healthy, and organized.

Let's speak of banks. We have excellent banking institutions. The banks today manage all the resources for all the expenses of the nation; they payout in accordance with the established programs. You will never see the director of any bank out to lunch with the representative of some powerful corporation. Directors are never invited to dine in a restaurant or travel to Europe and stay in the owner's house or some luxurious hotel. Some of our businessmen make million-dollar deals, and the fine art of corruption as it is practised in capitalist circles is as subtle as a serpent and worse than a rat. They will anaesthetize you while you are being 'bitten', and they can rip off a chunk of flesh in the middle of the night. This was the way the Revolution was being put to sleep so that a piece of flesh could then be ripped away. In a few cases, corruption was out in the open. Many knew about its existence or suspected it when they observed the lifestyle changes, the new car, the house being redecorated, adding little decorative touches here and there because of pure vanity. We have heard such stories time and time again, and measures must be taken even though they will not be resolved easily.

The sugar industry once produced 8 million tonnes, and today this figure barely reaches 1.5 tonnes. We had to radically cut back on tilling and seeding the land while oil was costing forty dollars a barrel; it was ruinous for the country, particularly if you added to the equation the hurricanes that were passing through with increasing frequency, the prolonged droughts, and because the cane fields had a life span of four or five years when once they lasted for fifteen or more, and when the market price was 7 cents. I remember that one day I asked a company that sells our sugar about the price and production of sugar at the end of March, and they didn't even know how much sugar was being produced for months, much less the cost of a tonne of sugar in US dollars; I received the answer about a month and a half later.

Quite simply, we had to shut down sugar mills, or we were going to disappear down the Bartlett Trench. The country had many, many economists, and it is not my intention to criticize them, but speaking with the same honesty I used to describe the errors of the Revolution, I would like to ask why we hadn't discovered that maintaining production levels of sugar would be impossible. The USSR had collapsed. Oil was costing forty dollars a barrel; sugar prices were at basement levels; so why did we not rationalize that industry instead of sowing 20,000 caballerias that year, the equivalent of almost 270,000 hectares, thus obliging us to till the land with tractors and heavy ploughs, sowing cane that afterwards had to be cleaned using machinery, fertilized with expensive herbicides, etc. None of our economists seemed to have noticed any of this, and we practically had to instruct them, order them, to stop the procedure. It is like saying: 'The country is being invaded'; you cannot reply: 'Hold on, let me have thirty meetings with hundreds of people'. It's as if we had said in Giron: 'Let's hold a meeting for three days to discuss what we should do to repel the invasion'. Throughout its history, I assure you that the Revolution has been a constant and real war, with the enemy stalking us and ready to strike at us if we should let down our guard.

I called the minister and told him: Tell me please, how many hectares are ploughed?' The answer: 'Eighty thousand.' My response was: 'Not one hectare more'. That wasn't really up to me, but I had no option; you just can't let the country go down the tubes, and in April, I was looking at 20,000 caballerias of land being ploughed.

We have had to do many more things like this, things that would make the stones speak. It's not your fault, but what was happening to us? Why did we not see all this? The USSR had already collapsed; overnight, we had been left without oil, without raw materials, without food, without cleaning products, without anything. Probably, it was good that this happened, after all. Maybe we needed to suffer as we did so that we are ready to give our lives a hundred times over before we surrender the country or the Revolution—the Revolution we so deeply believe in.

Maybe it was all necessary, for we have committed many errors; we are trying to correct these errors; we are in the process of correcting them.

Let there never be a situation like the USSR here, or broken, dispersed socialist blocks! The empire shall not come here to set up secret jails to torture progressive men and women from other parts of this continent that are today rising up to fight for the second and final independence!

Rather than return to live such a repugnant and miserable life, it would be preferable to erase even the slightest trace of the memory of our descendants or us.

I said that we are more and more revolutionary, and I said this for a reason. Now, we understand the empire better and better; we are increasingly aware of what it is capable of; while before, we were sceptical about some things, they seemed to us impossible.

They had fooled the world. When the mass media grew in full

force, it took control of peoples' minds and exercised its power not only through lies but also through conditioned response. A lie isn't the same as a conditioned response: a lie affects one's knowledge, whereas the conditioned response affects one's ability to think. And being misinformed isn't the same as having lost the ability to think, because responses have been created for you: 'This is bad, that is bad; socialism is bad, socialism is bad', they say, and all the ignorant people and all the humble people and all the exploited people are saying: 'Socialism is bad'. And all the poor people, all the exploited people, and all the illiterate people are repeating it: 'Communism is bad'. 'Cuba is bad, Cuba is bad', the empire has said it; it has been said in Geneva; it has been said all over the place; and all the exploited people around the world, all the illiterate people and all those who don't receive medical care, or education or have any guarantee of a job, or of anything are saying: 'The Cuban Revolution is bad, the Cuban Revolution is bad. Listen, the Cuban Revolution did this and that'. But listen to this too: 'No-one is illiterate in Cuba'. Listen, 'the infant mortality rate is such and such'. Listen, 'everyone can read and write'. Listen, 'freedom can't exist without culture'. Listen, 'there can't be a choice'.

What are they talking about? What can illiterate people do? How can they know if the International Monetary Fund is good or bad, that the interest rate is higher, or that the world is being ceaselessly subjugated and pillaged by a thousand different methods put into practice by this system? They don't know.

They don't teach the masses to read and write; yet, they spend a million dollars on publicity every year. But it isn't the fact that they spend it; it's the fact that they spend it on creating conditioned responses because someone bought Palmolive, someone else bought Colgate, and someone else bought Candado soap, and just because they were told to do so, a hundred times over, they associated the products with a pretty image, this sowed its seed and carved its place in the brain. They who talk so much about brainwashing, it is they who carve their place, mould the brain, and take away from the human being his capacity to think. It would be less severe if they were taking away the ability to think from someone who had been to university, who could read a book.

What can the illiterate read? What means have they of realizing that they are being conned? What means have they of knowing that the biggest lie in the world is the one that claims that the rotten system that reigns over there, and in many places, if not almost all the countries that copied that system, is a democracy? The damage that they are doing is terrible. Day after day, people are becoming aware of this, and day after day, they feel more disdain, more disgust, more hatred, more condemnation, and a greater desire to fight. This is what, in the end, makes everyone much more revolutionary than they were when they were unaware of many of these things when they only knew about elements of injustice and inequality.

While I'm talking to you about this, I'm not theorizing; although it is necessary to theorize, we are working; we are moving towards complete changes in our society. We have to change again because we have gone through some challenging times, and these inequalities and injustices have arisen, and we are going to change this situation without abusing anyone's rights in the least and without taking money away from anyone. No, we're not going to take anybody's money; in our eyes, the faith that our people have in the bank is the most important thing of all. The Revolution is creating wealth, and because the Revolution is going to create a significant input that isn't derived from the sugar industry or any of that, it will mainly come from that capital, and also from experience, because knowing what must be done is very important.

What bitterness there was that day when the dollar shops opened, as a means to collect a little bit of the remittance money, and those with this money went to spend it in those shops that were expensive and aimed at collecting a bit of this money and redistributing it to those who didn't get any, at a time when the country was in a very difficult situation.

One day we asked and were told that in some provinces, 30 or 40 per cent of the people receive something, a little, but sending over a dollar is a good deal, an excellent deal! So good that it could easily ruin us because of the enormous purchasing power they have in a blockaded country, with highly subsidized rationed products and free or amazingly cheap services.

I really had no intention of getting involved in a dissertation on such sensitive matters. Still, it would have been a crime not to take advantage of the moment and tell you some of the things related to the economy, to the material life of the country, to the future of the Revolution, to revolutionary ideas, to the reasons why we began this struggle, to the colossal strength we possess today, the country we are today and may continue to be, which is much more than we are now.

I could never show my face again if I were lying or exaggerating; I prefer to do things rather than make promises. In any case, I do not do anything because a man alone cannot do a thing. I avail myself of the experience or the authority with which I have to wage this battle. There are millions of Cubans ready to wage this war, which is a war of all the people.

I mentioned that we have reached military invulnerability, that this empire cannot afford the price of the lives that would be lost, numbering as many or more than in Vietnam, if they try to occupy our land. The US people are unwilling to allow their leaders to waste thousands of lives on their imperial quests. Let's see if the tally reaches 3,000 in Iraq; it is at 2,000 already, and daily, the news is grimmer for those who started that war.

And let's see what will happen with this dirty blockade. Many people in the US are upset because they couldn't accept the help of our Cuban doctors; the majority were in favour and the local authorities more so.

Let's see, because we can show them that it would be better to get rid of that trash because it will never destroy our Revolution. We can tell Europe: Keep your humanitarian aid, you hypocrites, keep it all because we don't need it. What a wonderful thing it is to be able to say that we do not need help from Europe or the empire! Finish it whenever you want, even though we don't care if you do or not, because we have learned how to save, think, and grow; we have learned to multiply our efforts so that we can rise to the challenge of our colossal adversary.

Salvador Allende once spoke of things that would happen sooner rather than later. I believe that sooner rather than later, the empire will disintegrate. The people of the United States will enjoy more freedom than ever; they will be able to aspire to more justice than ever; they will be able to use science and technology for their improvement and the betterment of humanity; they will be able to join all of us who fight for the survival of the species; and they will be able to join all of us who fight for opportunities for the human species.

It's only fair to struggle for that, and that is why we must use all our energy, all our effort, and all our time to be able to say with the voice of millions, or hundreds of thousands of millions of people: It is worthwhile to have been born! It is worthwhile to have lived!

Contributors

FERNANDO GONZALEZ LLORT is one of the 'Cuban Five', the revolutionary heroes, unfairly imprisoned in the United States for fighting against terrorist organizations that have operated from US territory against Cuba. In 2017 he was appointed President of Cuba's Institute for Friendship with the Peoples (ICAP). A graduate of International Relations, Fernando served as an internationalist combatant in southern Angola between 1987–89.

FIDEL CASTRO RUZ (13 August 1926 – 25 November 2016) was the leader of the Cuban Revolution. He was for many years the First Secretary of the Communist Party of Cuba and President of the Republic of Cuba.

MANOLO DE LOS SANTOS is Co-Executive Director of The People's Forum and researcher at Tricontinental: Institute for Social Research. He co-edited, most recently, *Viviremos: Venezuela vs Hybrid War* (LeftWord 2020).

VIJAY PRASHAD is Executive Director of Tricontinental: Institute for Social Research, and editor at LeftWord Books. He is the author and/or editor of numerous books, including, most recently, *Washington Bullets* (LeftWord 2020).